Vegan Recipes: 100 Delicious Slow Cooker Recipes

Cooker Recipes

The Essential Vegan Diet Slow Cooker Cookbook

Anthony Haden

Elevate Publishing Limited

The material on this book is for informational purposes only. As each individual situation is unique, you should use proper discretion, in consultation with a health care practitioner, before undertaking the protocols, diet, exercises, techniques, training methods, or otherwise described herein. The author and publisher expressly disclaim responsibility for any adverse effects that may result from the use or application of the information contained herein.

Table of Contents

5

Introduction to Veganism for Beginners

The term vegan is thrown around a lot these days. You have probably heard of it yourself, and you may have even wondered exactly what it means. Veganism started as a diet, where those who ate according to it would avoid any and all animal products and byproducts. That means anything that comes from an animal (meat, eggs, dairy, etc.) are off of the menu for these individuals.

The word vegan can be used as an adjective, or a noun. People use it to describe their way of eating, or their way of life, as well as to describe themselves as a person. When someone says they are vegan, it can mean one of a few things: either they eat a vegan diet, or they follow a vegan lifestyle.

The differences between a vegan diet and a vegan lifestyle are minimal, but important. Those who follow the vegan diet are the individuals who apply all of the rules of animal welfare to their eating habits. That is, nothing that could potentially harm or exploit animals will be a part of their diet. Individuals who live a vegan lifestyle will extend this rule beyond their eating habits and into other areas of life. That means they won't purchase anything (clothes, décor, cooking accessories, etc.) that could have potentially caused harm to or exploited any animals. Many times, these individuals will also avoid anything that exploits or harms humans, as well. They do not support any brands that use cheap labor, child labor, slavery, or any other means of inappropriate or non-ideal labor to achieve the creation of their products.

For this book, we are going to focus on the vegan diet. Many people choose it for ethical reasons, but many others choose it for the health benefits it has. In the next part of this chapter, we are going to explore the various reasons why anyone would choose to eat a vegan diet.

Why Should I Go Vegan?

There are several reasons as to why anyone would choose to go vegan. Not only is it a nutritious and delicious way of life, but it also boasts many wonderful benefits, which we will discuss more later in this book.

Some reasons why people choose veganism includes: morals, ethical reasons, environmental concerns, and health purposes. Some of the positive side effects of eating a vegan diet include: less animals being exposed to unfit living conditions, increased animal welfare, more food to feed the hungry, sustainable farming practices that benefit the environment, and more. When people eat vegan, not only are they promoting a healthier body, but they are also promoting a healthier, kinder planet for all involved.

Veganism is great to achieve many things. You can be proud for supporting all of the above, while also supporting your own health. When you eat a vegan diet, you reduce your risk of contracting many different illnesses, diseases and ailments. You can also lessen the severity of symptoms and conditions you already live with. In addition, you will see significant increase in your physical health, stamina, and libido, as well as your mental health and wellbeing. The vegan diet is an incredible way of eating that has so much to offer you, and the world around you.

Slower Cook Do's and Don'ts

DO's

Follow Cooking Times —If you have to work all day and want to make a recipe that has a shorter cooking time, purchase a programmable slow cooker that switches to warm once cooking is complete. This will make each meal the best quality it can be, no matter how much time it takes.

Use the Right Size Slow Cooker —Most recipes in this book work best using a 5 to 6-quart slow cooker. If you have a different size cooker, keep a close eye on cooking times and monitor the meal to make sure that the finished product is not overcooked.

Prep Your Slow Cooker – Some recipes may call for prepping your slow cooker with cooking spray before cooking. If this is the case, overlook the simple steps. Otherwise, this could end up being a mess to clean up afterwards.

Cook On Low – Some recipes in this book will include options for cooking food on low or high, depending on your time schedule. It is recommended to keep heat on low to create most dishes

Plan Ahead – One of the benefits of slow cooking is the amount of time it saves. To save time in the morning, prep vegetables the night before and store them in separate containers in the refrigerator. Then, in the morning, all you have to do is add the ingredients and set the slow cooker to the appropriate time .

DON'Ts

Remove the Lid While Cooking – Although sometimes it may be necessary to look inside your slow cooker to see its progress, taking off the lid can affect the overall cooking time as it takes quite a while to heat the slow cooker back up once the lid is removed. If you need to look inside the cooker, as a rule of thumb you should add an additional 30 to 40 minutes to the overall cooking time.

Overfill the Slow Cooker – Slow cookers are usually designed to be filled to no more than two thirds. Keep this in mind when you're using your slow cooker as it can greatly affect cooking times. Make sure to check your manufacturer's instructions before you start cooking.

Benefits of a Slower Cooker

To me, having a good slow cooker is one of the must-have tools when you're on a diet. Not only does it save time, but it makes cooking healthy meals incredibly easy! Here are some of the other many benefits of using a slow cooker:

More nutrient rich food - When foods are cooked normally, they lose many of their vitamins and minerals. However, when foods are cooked in crockpots, they retain much more of their vitamins and minerals. This is because food is cooked at a much lower heat for a longer time and high heat destroys nutrients.

Saves money - Slow cookers helps you save money in two ways. They use less energy than a stove or oven.

Less clean up - Since you're only using a slow cooker to make your food, the time you spend on cleaning up will be much less than with conventional methods.

Measurement Conversion Note

Some recipes in this book have ingredients that are given in metric units, and it's important to get the right amount of ingredients in your meal creations.

Here is a quick and easy measurement conversion breakdown:

8 Ounces (Metric) = 1 Cup (US)
1 Ounce (Metric) = 1/8 Cup (US)
1 Ounce (Metric) = 28.35 Grams

Now that you're sold on all the benefits of using a slow cooker, let's take a look at all the delicious vegan recipes you can make with it!

Vegan Slow Cooker Recipes

Breakfast

Apple Bread

Prep Time: 20 minutes; **Cook Time:** 2-2 1/2 hours on HIGH
Serving Size: 105 g; **Serves:** 14-16; **Calories:** 328
Total Fat: 9.8 g **Saturated Fat:** 5 g; **Trans Fat:** 0 g
Protein: 4.9 g; **Total Carbs:** 56.4 g
Dietary Fiber: 2 g; **Sugars:** 26.4 g
Cholesterol: 17 mg; **Sodium:** 931 mg; **Potassium:** 160 mg;
Vitamin A: 4%; **Vitamin C:** 3%; **Calcium:** 3%; **Iron:** 12%

Ingredients:
- ☐ 1 1/2 cups cooking apples, peeled and diced
- ☐ 1 tablespoon ground cinnamon
- ☐ 1 teaspoon vanilla
- ☐ 1/2 cup Earth Balance buttery spread, melted
- ☐ 1/3 cup apple cider
- ☐ 1/4 teaspoon ground ginger
- ☐ 3/4 cup brown sugar, packed
- ☐ 3/4 cup granulated sugar
- ☐ 4 cans (7 1/2 ounces each) vegan refrigerated biscuits (40 biscuits total)
- ☐ Pinch ground nutmeg OR few grates fresh nutmeg

Directions:
1. Grease a 4-quart slow cooker with nonstick cooking spray. In a large-sized bowl, mix the brown sugar with the granulated sugar, nutmeg, cinnamon, and ginger. Sprinkle the bottom of the cooker with 2 tablespoons of the sugar mix. Set aside the remaining sugar mixture
2. Cut each biscuit into quarters. Add the apples and the biscuit quarters into the bowl with the sugar mixture; toss to coat. Add the mix into the cooker. Sprinkle the apple mix with any remaining sugar mixture.
3. In a small-sized bowl, stir the apple cider with the vegan butter and vanilla. Pour the mix over the biscuits.

4. Cover and cook for 2 to 2 1/2 hours on HIGH or until comes out clean when inserted in the center of the apple bread. When the bread is cooked, turn off the slow cooker. Carefully open the lid to prevent the condensation from dripping onto the bread. Cover the opening of the cooker paper towels and then set the lid on top. Let the bread cool for about 10-15 minutes. When cooled, run a knife around the edges of the bread. Transfer the bread onto a serving platter. Spoon any remaining topping from the cooker on top of the bread and let cool until warm enough to eat. Serve.

Pumpkin Oatmeal

Prep Time: 5 minutes; **Cook Time:** 8 hours, 5 minutes
Serving Size: 262 g; **Serves:** 4; **Calories:** 106
Total Fat: 1.5 g **Saturated Fat:** 0 g; **Trans Fat:** 0 g
Protein: 3.4 g; **Total Carbs:** 19.4 g
Dietary Fiber: 4 g; **Sugars:** 2.5 g
Cholesterol: 0 mg; **Sodium:** 49 mg; **Potassium:** 208 mg;
Vitamin A: 191%; **Vitamin C:** 4%; **Calcium:** 5%; **Iron:** 10%

Ingredients:

- ☐ 1 cup pumpkin puree (not pie filling)
- ☐ 1 cup steel cut oats OR Coach's Oats
- ☐ 1 pinch salt
- ☐ 1/2 teaspoon cinnamon, ground
- ☐ 1/2 teaspoon pumpkin pie spice
- ☐ 2 teaspoons vanilla extract
- ☐ 3 cups water
- ☐ 1 teaspoon stevia, or to taste, optional

Directions:

1. Take a heat-safe bowl that will fit your slow cooker. Put all the ingredients in the bowl and stir to combine. Place the bowl in the slow cooker. Pour just enough water into the slow cooker until the water level comes to half the height of the bowl.
2. Cover cook for 6-8 hours on LOW.
3. When cooked, serve with maple syrup, brown sugar, pat of vegan butter, pumpkin seeds, cranberries, or nuts.

Sri Lankan Kiri Bath a.k.a Savory Creamy Coconut Milk Rice

Prep Time: 15 minutes;	**Cook Time:** 3 hours on LOW

Serving Size: 137 g; **Serves:** 12; **Calories:** 265

Total Fat: 16 g **Saturated Fat:** 14 g; **Trans Fat:** 0 g

Protein: 3.7 g; **Total Carbs:** 28.3 g

Dietary Fiber: 1.9 g; **Sugars:** 2.2 g

Cholesterol: 0 mg; **Sodium:** 24 mg; **Potassium:** 210 mg;

Vitamin A: 0%; **Vitamin C:** 3%; **Calcium:** 2%; **Iron:** 13%

Ingredients:
- ☐ 2 cans (14-15 ounces each) coconut milk, unsweetened (do not use sweetened coconut cream or milk)
- ☐ 2 cups white rice (do not use basmati), plain or mixed with some Sri Red Rice
- ☐ 2-3 cups water, or as needed
- ☐ Salt, to taste

Directions:
1. Rinse the rice well. Put all the ingredients into the slow cooker. Cover and cook for 3 hours on LOW.
2. Check after 2 1/2 hours if the rice is tender and cooked through. If needed, add 1 cup more cup of water. The consistency should be thick and creamy, similar to a thick rice pudding.
3. When the rice is cooked, let the rice pudding cool covered for 30 minutes.
4. Serve this dish with your favorite Sri-Lankan-inspired meal for breakfast.

Breakfast Apple Crumble Pudding

Prep Time: 10 minutes; **Cook Time:** 4 hours on LOW, 2 hours on HIGH

Serving Size: 232 g; **Serves:** 6; **Calories:** 186

Total Fat: 6 g **Saturated Fat:** 1.3 g; **Trans Fat**: 0 g

Protein: 2.6 g; **Total Carbs:** 36.2 g

Dietary Fiber: 7.4 g; **Sugars:** 24.4 g

Cholesterol: 0 mg; **Sodium:** 63 mg; **Potassium:** 333 mg;

Vitamin A: 0%; **Vitamin C:** 24%; **Calcium:** 9%; **Iron:** 11%

Ingredients:
For the pudding:
- ☐ 5 apples, large-sized, unpeeled, sliced
- ☐ 2 tablespoons maple syrup
- ☐ 2 tablespoons arrowroot powder
- ☐ 2 cups water
- ☐ 1/2 cup chia seeds
- ☐ 1 teaspoon ground cinnamon
- ☐ 1 cup unsweetened almond milk, or your preferred non-dairy milk
- ☐ Pinch Himalayan rock salt

For the cinnamon crunch topping:
- ☐ 1/4 cup apple sauce, unsweetened
- ☐ 1/4 cup shredded coconut, unsweetened
- ☐ 1/4 cup coconut sugar
- ☐ 1/2 cup blanched almond flour
- ☐ 1 teaspoon pure vanilla extract
- ☐ 1 teaspoon cinnamon

Directions:
1. In the bottom of a 3-quart slow cooker, mix the milk with the maple syrup, water, arrowroot, chia, salt, and cinnamon.
2. Layer the apple slices on top of the milk mix – do not stir or combine.
3. In a large-sized bowl, mix all the crumble topping ingredients together. With your hands, spread the crumble mix on top of the apples.

4. Cover and cook for 4 hours on LOW or for 2 hours on HIGH. I like the cooked results of the low setting, but either cooking setting works.
5. After desired cooking time, turn off the slow cooker and unplug. Let the crumble pudding sit for 1 hour.
6. Top each serving with walnuts and raisins. Serve with couple pieces dried fruits and your favorite non-dairy milk.

Notes: If you don't have arrowroot powder, you can use cornstarch, tapioca starch, or potato starch to slightly thicken the pudding. You can boost the protein content of this dish by adding protein powder into the milk mixture.

Pumpkin Granola

Prep Time: 15 minutes; **Cook Time:** 4 hours on HIGH	
Serving Size: 84 g; **Serves:** 12; **Calories:** 238	
Total Fat: 7.6 g **Saturated Fat:** 1.4 g; **Trans Fat:** 0 g	
Protein: 7.5 g; **Total Carbs:** 36.5 g	
Dietary Fiber: 4.8 g; **Sugars:** 9.1 g	
Cholesterol: 0 mg; **Sodium:** 154 mg; **Potassium:** 294 mg;	
Vitamin A: 49%; **Vitamin C:** 6%; **Calcium:** 4%; **Iron:** 21%	

Ingredients:
- ☐ 5 cups rolled oats, certified gluten-free
- ☐ 3/4 teaspoon kosher salt
- ☐ 3/4 cup pumpkin puree, canned
- ☐ 1/2- 3/4 cup maple syrup (start with the smaller amount)
- ☐ 1 teaspoon ground cinnamon
- ☐ 1 tablespoon pumpkin pie spice
- ☐ 1 cup dried cranberries and/or raisins
- ☐ 1 cup almonds, whole OR pumpkin seeds, toasted

Directions:
1. Except for the dried fruits, put all the ingredients in a 6 1/2-quart slow cooker and stir to combine. Mix well because the maple will be gloppy.
2. Cover and cook for 4 hours on HIGH vented. If your slow cooker does not have a vent, prop the lid open using a wooden spoon or a chopstick. Stir the mixture every 30

minutes or so. Cook until the granola reaches your desired consistency and texture.

3. When cooked, spread the mixture on paper towels or foil and let cool completely. The granola will become crispier and harder as they cool.
4. When cooled, mix in the cranberries. Store in airtight containers and keep in the freezer or in the fridge.
5. Serve with your favorite vegan yogurt.

Overnight Maple Oatmeal

Prep Time: 5 minutes; **Cook Time:** 7-8 hours on LOW	

Prep Time: 5 minutes; **Cook Time:** 7-8 hours on LOW

Serving Size: 284 g; **Serves:** 6-8; **Calories:** 162

Total Fat: 1.8 g **Saturated Fat:** 0 g; **Trans Fat:** 0 g

Protein: 3.6 g; **Total Carbs:** 33.5 g

Dietary Fiber: 3 g; **Sugars:** 14 g

Cholesterol: 0 mg; **Sodium:** 205 mg; **Potassium:** 138 mg;

Vitamin A: 0%; **Vitamin C:** 0%; **Calcium:** 4%; **Iron:** 8%

Ingredients:
- ☐ 2 cups steel cut oats
- ☐ 1/4 cup pure maple syrup
- ☐ 1/4 cup light brown sugar, packed
- ☐ 1/2 teaspoon salt
- ☐ 1 teaspoon ground cinnamon
- ☐ 6-8 cups water
- ☐ 3/4 cup dried blueberries, optional

Directions:
1. Lightly grease a 4 to 5-quart slow cooker with cooking spray. Put all of the ingredients in the cooker and stir to combine.
2. Cover and cook for 7-8 hours on LOW. When cooked, stir thoroughly using a wooden spoon or rubber spatula. Serve immediately.

Notes: Portions leftovers in a containers and keep refrigerated for up to 3 to 4 days. Just reheat when ready to serve.

Pumpkin Spice Latte

Prep Time: 25 minutes;	**Cook Time:** 7 to 9 hours on LOW

Serving Size: 513 g; **Serves:** 1; **Calories:** 779

Total Fat: 47.8 g **Saturated Fat:** 42.1 g; **Trans Fat:** 0 g

Protein: 6.2 g; **Total Carbs:** 93.1 g

Dietary Fiber: 8.4 g; **Sugars:** 81 g

Cholesterol: 0 mg; **Sodium:** 59 mg; **Potassium:** 941 mg;

Vitamin A: 381%; **Vitamin C:** 18%; **Calcium:** 13%; **Iron:** 31%

Ingredients:

For the latte:

- ☐ 1/2 cup brewed coffee, really strong OR 1 shot espresso
- ☐ 3-4 tablespoons pumpkin spice syrup, recipe below
- ☐ 6 ounces almond milk OR your preferred non-dairy milk
- ☐ Fresh grated nutmeg

For the pumpkin spice syrup (makes 2 servings):

- ☐ 1 can (14-ounces) coconut milk, full-fat
- ☐ 1 cup pumpkin puree, organic
- ☐ 1 cup light brown sugar, packed
- ☐ 1/8 teaspoon ground cardamom
- ☐ 1/8 teaspoon ground allspice
- ☐ 1/2 teaspoon ground ginger
- ☐ 1/2 teaspoon ground cinnamon
- ☐ Pinch cloves

Directions:

For the pumpkin spice syrup:

1. Put all the ingredients in the slow cooker and whisk well until combined. Cover and cook for 7 to 9 hours on LOW.
2. When cooked, whisk until thoroughly combined, breaking up any lumps in the process – store in the fridge for up to 1 week.

For the latte:

1. Over medium heat, heat the almond milk in a 2-quart saucepan. Let the milk heat until the edges simmer, but

do not bring to a boil. Remove the pan from the heat and place in a heat-safe flat surface.
2. Using an electric mixer, whip the milk, increasing the speed as it starts to thicken. Continue to whip until the milk is frothy.
3. Put 3 to 4 tablespoons of the prepared pumpkin spice syrup into a coffee cup. Pour 1 shot of espresso into the cup and gently stir using a spoon to mix. Gently pour milk into the cup, holding back the froth using a spoon. Pour enough milk until the mix is 1/4 inch full from the top of the cup. Spoon mounds of foam on top of the latter. Sprinkle with fresh ground nutmeg.

Coconut Milk Steel Cut Oats

Prep Time: 10 minutes; **Cook Time:** 8 hours	
Serving Size: 410 g; **Serves**: 6-8; **Calories**: 258	
Total Fat: 17.6 g **Saturated Fat:** 14.3 g; **Trans Fat**: 0 g	
Protein: 5.1 g; **Total Carbs:** 22.2 g	
Dietary Fiber: 4.2 g; **Sugars:** 2.6 g	
Cholesterol: 0 mg; **Sodium:** 21 mg; **Potassium**: 277 mg;	
Vitamin A: 0%; **Vitamin C**: 3%; **Calcium**: 3%; **Iron**: 12%	

Ingredients:
- ☐ 1 can (14 ounces) coconut milk, full fat
- ☐ 1 teaspoon vanilla
- ☐ 2 cups steel cut oatmeal
- ☐ 8 cups water
- ☐ 2 tablespoons coconut sugar, optional

Directions:
1. Put all of the ingredients in the slow cooker.
2. Cover and cook for 8 hours on LOW or until the dish is creamy.
3. Serve with your favorite nut butter, chia seeds, dried fruit, raisins, pumpkin seeds, coconut flakes, or your choice of toppings.

Pumpkin Butter

Prep Time: 5 minutes; **Cook Time:** 5-6 hours on LOW

Serving Size: 30 g; **Serves:** 44 tablespoons; **Calories:** 32

Total Fat: 0.1 g **Saturated Fat:** 0 g; **Trans Fat:** 0 g

Protein: 0.2 g; **Total Carbs:** 8 g

Dietary Fiber: 0.6 g; **Sugars:** 6.3 g

Cholesterol: 0 mg; **Sodium:** 14 mg; **Potassium:** 63 mg;

Vitamin A: 60%; **Vitamin C:** 2%; **Calcium:** 1%; **Iron:** 2%

Ingredients:
- [ ] 2 cans (15-ounce each) pumpkin (about 4 cups of fresh)
- [ ] 2 tablespoons lemon juice
- [ ] 1/4 teaspoon salt
- [ ] 1/2 teaspoon nutmeg
- [ ] 1/2 teaspoon cinnamon
- [ ] 1/2 cup apple juice
- [ ] 1 teaspoon ground ginger
- [ ] 1 1/4 cups maple syrup

Directions:
1. Put all of the ingredients into the slow cooker and stir to combine.
2. Cover and cook for 5-6 hours on LOW.
3. When the cooking time is up, let it cool for at least 1 hour and refrigerate overnight.
4. Serve with your favorite breakfast bread.

Notes: You can store this butter in canning jars and keep in the refrigerator for 1 week or freeze for 6 months.

Blueberry Butter

Prep Time: 15 minutes; **Cook Time:** 5 hours on LOW, plus 1 hour on HIGH	
Serving Size: 38 g; **Serves:** 32 tablespoons; **Calories:** 42	
Total Fat: 0.1 g **Saturated Fat:** 0 g; **Trans Fat:** 0 g	
Protein: 0.2 g; **Total Carbs:** 11 g	
Dietary Fiber: 0.9 g; **Sugars:** 9.4 g	
Cholesterol: 0 mg; **Sodium:** 0 mg; **Potassium:** 25 mg;	
Vitamin A: 0%; **Vitamin C:** 8%; **Calcium:** 0%; **Iron:** 3%	

Ingredients:
- [ ] 36 ounces blueberries, pureed (about 5 cups pureed)
- [ ] 2 teaspoons cinnamon
- [ ] 1 lemon, zested
- [ ] 1 teaspoon dried lavender, optional
- [ ] 1 cup sugar
- [ ] 1/4 teaspoon ground ginger, optional
- [ ] 1/2 teaspoon ground nutmeg, optional

Directions:
1. Put the pureed blueberries into the slow cooker. Cook for 1 hour on LOW. Stir the pureed blueberry. If using dried lavender, put the lavender in a bouquet garni bag and tie it close. Put the bag lavender in the slow cooker.
2. Prop the lid of the slow cooker using a wooden spoon or a spatula. Cook for 4 more hours on LOW. Add the sugar, lemon zest, and spices. Stir to combine.
3. If the puree is not thickened, remove the lid of slow cooker and cook for 1 hour on HIGH. Remove and discard the bag of lavender.
4. Pour the butter in a blender or food processor and puree until smooth. Store in airtight containers or processed jars.
5. To store in processed jars, pour the butter into sterilized jars, leaving 1/2 inch of space from the top of the jars. Wipe the rims clean and screw the lids. Process for 10 minutes in boiling water canner and store the jars in dark, cool place.
6. Serve with your favorite bread.

Italian Eggplant Casserole with Cashew-Tofu Ricotta

Prep Time: 30 minutes; **Cook Time:** 6-8 hours on LOW

Serving Size: 335 g; **Serves:** 6; **Calories:** 295

Total Fat: 12.7 g **Saturated Fat:** 2.6 g; **Trans Fat:** 0 g

Protein: 16.9 g; **Total Carbs:** 33.6 g

Dietary Fiber: 10.9 g; **Sugars:** 14.3 g

Cholesterol: 2 mg; **Sodium:** 714 mg; **Potassium:** 1103 mg;

Vitamin A: 11%; **Vitamin C:** 10%; **Calcium:** 22%; **Iron:** 31%

Ingredients:

- ☐ 1 eggplant, large-sized (about 1 1/4 pounds), thinly sliced with a mandolin into 1/4-inch thick
- ☐ 1 jar (25 ounces or 700 grams) marinara sauce, homemade or store-bought (I used tomato basil sauce)
- ☐ Cooked vegan pasta, for serving

For the cashew-tofu ricotta:
- ☐ 1 package (15 ounces) firm tofu
- ☐ 1/2 cup cashews (2 ounces or 56 grams)
- ☐ 1/2 cup nutritional yeast
- ☐ 1/2 cup unsweetened non-dairy milk
- ☐ 1/2 teaspoon salt
- ☐ 2 teaspoons lemon juice
- ☐ 3 cloves garlic
- ☐ Fresh ground black pepper, to taste

Directions:

The night before:
1. Make the vegan ricotta cheese. Put all the ingredients in a blender or a food processor until smooth. Store in a covered container and keep in the refrigerator.

In the morning:
1. Lightly grease the slow cooker with cooking spray.
2. Pour 1/3 of the marinara sauce into the cooker. Top the marinara sauce with 1/2 of the eggplant slices, 1/2 of the ricotta, and then 1/3 of the marinara sauce. Repeat the

layers with the top layer with the remaining marinara sauce.
3. Cover and cook for 6 to 8 hours on LOW.
4. Serve with pasta.

Lunch

Pinto Beans, Corn, and Chipotle Tacos

Prep Time: 20 minutes; **Cook Time:** 3-4 hours on LOW; 1 1/2-2 hours on HIGH

Serving Size: 377 g; **Serves:** 4; **Calories:** 838
Total Fat: 3.4 g **Saturated Fat**: 0.8 g; **Trans Fat**: 0 g
Protein: 53 g; **Total Carbs:** 151.3 g;
Dietary Fiber: 35.7 g; **Sugars:** 18.1 g
Cholesterol: 3 mg; **Sodium:** 1575 mg; **Potassium:** 3737 mg;
Vitamin A: 22%; **Vitamin C**: 139%; **Calcium**: 46%; **Iron**: 73%

Ingredients:
- [ ] 1 can (6 ounces) tomato paste
- [ ] 1 chipotle pepper in adobo sauce, chopped
- [ ] 1 cup corn kernels, frozen, fresh, or canned
- [ ] 2 cans (15 ounces each) pinto beans, drained
- [ ] 1/2 teaspoon salt
- [ ] 1/2 teaspoon ground cinnamon
- [ ] 1 teaspoon ground cumin
- [ ] 1 tablespoon unsweetened cocoa powder
- [ ] 3/4 cup chili sauce

Directions:
1. Put all the ingredients in the slow cooker. Give them a good stir to combine.
2. Cover and cook for 3-4 hours on LOW or for 1 1/2-2 hours on HIGH.
3. Spread the mixture into your favorite soft or hard taco shells. Top with sliced lettuce. If desired, add fresh tomatoes, avocado, and fresh squeeze of lime juice.
4. You can even serve this with rice.

Notes: If making ahead of time, let the mixture cool to room temperature. Store them in rigid containers and freeze. When ready to spread, transfer into the refrigerator and let thaw for 4-6 hours. Put into a saucepan and heat through. Serve.

Lentil Barbecue Sandwich

Prep Time: 10 minutes; **Cook Time:** 4-5 hours on HIGH, 6-8 hours on LOW	
Serving Size: 265 g; **Serves:** 8-10; **Calories:** 472	
Total Fat: 1.3 g **Saturated Fat:** 0 g; **Trans Fat:** 0 g	
Protein: 28.4 g; **Total Carbs:** 88 g	
Dietary Fiber: 33.7 g; **Sugars:** 23.3 g	
Cholesterol: 0 mg; **Sodium:** 374 mg; **Potassium:** 1471 mg;	
Vitamin A: 28%; **Vitamin C:** 29%; **Calcium:** 16%; **Iron:** 58%	

Ingredients:
For the lentils:
- ☐ 2 cups green lentils
- ☐ 4 cups water

For the barbecue sauce:
- ☐ 6 ounces tomato paste, canned
- ☐ 28 ounces crushed tomatoes, canned
- ☐ 3 garlic cloves
- ☐ 2 tablespoons apple cider vinegar
- ☐ 1/8 teaspoon cayenne
- ☐ 1/4-1/2 teaspoon liquid smoke
- ☐ 1/4 teaspoon red pepper flakes
- ☐ 1/4 cup white vinegar
- ☐ 1/2 teaspoon Himalayan rock salt
- ☐ 1/2 cup blackstrap molasses
- ☐ 1 teaspoon dry mustard
- ☐ 1 tablespoon coconut sugar
- ☐ 1 sweet onion, medium-sized, quartered

Directions:
For the sauce:
1. Put all the ingredients in a blender or a food processor and process until smooth. Transfer the pureed mixture into a medium saucepan.
2. Cover and bring to a boil over medium heat. When boiling, reduce the heat to low, cover, and simmer for 30 minutes.

3. Remove from the heat. Stir in the cooked lentils. Serve on top of buns or bread spread with apple butter. Or serve as a burger topping.

For the lentils:
1. Put the beans in the crockpot. Add water (if cooking more beans, follow the 1:2 ratio: 1 cup beans for every 2 cups water).
2. Cover and cook for 4 to 5 hours on HIGH or for 8 to 6 hours on LOW.

Notes: You can cook beans ahead of time. When cooked, let them cool completely and store in sterilized containers with tight lids. If not using for a couple of weeks, keep the containers in the freezer, just make sure you are using freezable containers.

Quinoa and Lentil Tacos

Prep Time: 15 minutes; **Cook Time:** 7-9 hours on LOW

Serving Size: 373 g; **Serves:** 2; **Calories:** 556

Total Fat: 15.1 g **Saturated Fat:** 3 g; **Trans Fat:** 0 g

Protein: 20.2 g; **Total Carbs:** 83.7 g

Dietary Fiber: 19.5 g; **Sugars:** 1.9 g

Cholesterol: 0 mg; **Sodium:** 263 mg; **Potassium:** 758 mg;

Vitamin A: 10%; **Vitamin C:** 6%; **Calcium:** 12%; **Iron:** 34%

Ingredients:
- ☐ 1/4 cup brown lentils
- ☐ 1/4 cup beluga lentils or more brown lentils
- ☐ 1/4 cup quinoa, rinsed
- ☐ 1/2 teaspoon chili powder
- ☐ 1/2 teaspoon smoked paprika
- ☐ 2 cloves garlic, minced
- ☐ 2 cups water
- ☐ 6 corn taco shells, hard or soft
- ☐ Salt and pepper, to taste

Directions:
1. Except for the pepper and salt to taste, put all of the ingredients into a 1 1/2 to 2-quart slow cooker.
2. Cover and cook for 7-9 hours on LOW.
3. Before serving, season to taste with salt and pepper.
4. Serve in taco shells with lettuce leaves, salsa, tomatoes, or any of your favorite taco toppings.

Bulgogi Jackfruit a.k.a Vegan Pulled Pork

Prep Time: 10 minutes; **Cook Time:** 6 hours on LOW, plus 1 hour on HIGH

Serving Size: 184 g; **Serves:** 12; **Calories:** 215

Total Fat: 4.9 g **Saturated Fat:** 0.7 g; **Trans Fat:** 0 g

Protein: 3.4 g; **Total Carbs:** 39.9 g

Dietary Fiber: 2.4 g; **Sugars:** 13.6 g

Cholesterol: 0 mg; **Sodium:** 975 mg; **Potassium:** 397 mg;

Vitamin A: 6%; **Vitamin C:** 14%; **Calcium:** 5%; **Iron:** 7%

Ingredients:

- [ ] 2 cans (20 ounces) young, green jackfruit in brine, rinsed and drained
- [ ] 1 green pear, cored and chopped
- [ ] 1 cup white wine or mirin
- [ ] 1 onion, medium-sized, peeled and sliced
- [ ] 1/2 cup agave nectar or maple syrup
- [ ] 1/2 cup tamari
- [ ] 1/2 cup water
- [ ] 1/4 cup coconut aminos (or soy sauce)
- [ ] 2 tablespoons fresh ginger, peeled and minced
- [ ] 4 tablespoons sesame oil
- [ ] 8 cloves garlic, peeled and chopped

Directions:

1. Put the jackfruit in the slow cooker. Add the remaining ingredients in the slow cooker and stir to combine.
2. Cover and cook for 6 hours on LOW.
3. After 6 hours, adjust the setting to HIGH and cook for 1 hour to let the jackfruit absorb the liquid.
4. With a frim spatula, break the jackfruit apart into pieces.

Vegetarian Fajitas

Prep Time: 15 minutes; **Cook Time:** 4 to 6 hours on LOW; 2 hours on HIGH	

Prep Time: 15 minutes; **Cook Time:** 4 to 6 hours on LOW; 2 hours on HIGH

Serving Size: 103 g; **Serves:** 8; **Calories:** 96

Total Fat: 3.8 g **Saturated Fat:** 0.7 g; **Trans Fat:** 0 g

Protein: 2.6 g; **Total Carbs:** 16 g

Dietary Fiber: 5.6 g; **Sugars:** 9.2 g

Cholesterol: 0 mg; **Sodium:** 24 mg; **Potassium:** 475 mg;

Vitamin A: 107%; **Vitamin C:** 116%; **Calcium:** 2%; **Iron:** 9%

Ingredients:

- ☐ 4 ounces canned diced green chilies
- ☐ 3 Roma tomatoes, diced
- ☐ 2 teaspoons cumin
- ☐ 2 teaspoons chili powder
- ☐ 1/4 teaspoon garlic salt
- ☐ 1/2 teaspoon dried oregano
- ☐ 1 red bell pepper, large-sized, seeded and sliced
- ☐ 1 onion, medium-sized, sliced
- ☐ 1 green bell pepper, large-sized, seeded and sliced
- ☐ 1 1/2 tablespoons vegetable oil

Directions:

1. Grease a slow cooker with a thin coat of nonstick cooking spray.
2. Add all of the ingredients into the cooker. With a larger-sized spoon, mix the veggies until they are well coated with the spices and oil.
3. Cover and cook for 4 to 6 hours on LOW or for 2 hours on HIGH.
4. Serve with black beans, cashew sour cream, avocado, and warmed tortillas.

Notes: You can serve this dish with a spread of black beans onto the center of each tortilla and top with the fajita to make a more filling dish.

Lentil, Mushroom, and Brown Rice-Stuffed Cabbage Rolls

Prep Time: 45 minutes; **Cook Time:** 8-10 hours on LOW; 4-5 hours on HIGH	
Serving Size: 513 g; **Serves:** 4; **Calories:** 664	
Total Fat: 16 g **Saturated Fat:** 2.5 g; **Trans Fat:** 0 g	
Protein: 23.6 g; **Total Carbs:** 110.3 g	
Dietary Fiber: 26.4 g; **Sugars:** 28.3 g	
Cholesterol: 3 mg; **Sodium:** 1032 mg; **Potassium:** 1687 mg;	
Vitamin A: 22%; **Vitamin C:** 122%; **Calcium:** 19%; **Iron:** 45%	

Ingredients:
- ☐ 1 cup brown lentils, cooked (1/2 cup uncooked)
- ☐ 1 cup brown rice, long-grain, cooked (1/3 cup uncooked)
- ☐ 1 head green cabbage, large outermost leaves removed
- ☐ 1 jar (24-ounce) marinara sauce (or 3 cups homemade marinara sauce)
- ☐ 2 ounces cremini mushrooms, diced (3-4 mushrooms, about 3/4 cup diced)
- ☐ 1 tablespoon olive oil
- ☐ 1/2 cup onion, diced (1/4 medium onion)
- ☐ 1/2 teaspoon kosher salt
- ☐ 1/4 cup golden raisins
- ☐ 1/4 cup pine nuts, toasted
- ☐ 1/4 cup water
- ☐ 2 cloves garlic, minced
- ☐ 2 tablespoons fresh dill, minced, plus more for serving

Directions:
1. Bring a large-sized pot filled with water to a rolling boil. Set a colander over a large-sized bowl. Drop the cabbage into the pot carefully. Boil for 5 minutes. After boiling, put the cabbage into the prepared colander. Let drain and cool slightly.
2. Remove the outer leaves and until you reach the inner leaves that are not pliable. Repeat the boiling process until you have 8 pliable cabbage leaves. Pat the leaves dry and set aside until ready to use.

3. In a medium-sized bowl, stir the lentils, mushrooms, rice, onion, raisins, pine nuts, dill, garlic, salt, and olive oil until well mixed.
4. In a 3 quart or larger-sized slow cooker, add the 1/4 cup of water and marinara sauce. Stir well to combine.
5. Set a pliable cabbage leaf onto a clean work surface with the outer side faced down. Spoon about 1/2 cup of the lentil mixture into the middle of the cabbage leaf. Fold the stem end 1/3 of the way up, then fold the sides, and continue rolling the leaf semi-tightly until it's completely rolled up. With the seam side faced down, place on top of the marinara sauce in the cooker.
6. Repeat the remaining process with the lentil mixture and lettuce leaves, piling them on top of each other.
7. Cover and cook for 8-10 hours on LOW or for 4-5 hours on HIGH.
8. To serve, spoon a bit of the marinara sauce and spread it on a plate. One at a time, carefully transfer the cabbage rolls onto the plate. Ladle additional 1-2 spoonful of marinara sauce over the cabbage rolls and, if desired, top with a couple sprigs of fresh dill.

Notes: To toast the pine nuts, put a medium-sized sauté pan over medium heat. Add the pine nuts in the pan. Stirring frequently, cook for about 4 to 5 minutes or until the nuts are fragrant. Cook carefully, making sure to watch to prevent the nuts from burning.

Black-Eyed Peas Sloppy

Prep Time: 15 minutes; **Cook Time:** 7-9 hours on LOW	

Serving Size: 566 g; **Serves:** 2; **Calories:** 333

Total Fat: 3.4 g **Saturated Fat:** 0.6 g; **Trans Fat:** 0 g

Protein: 12.7 g; **Total Carbs:** 65 g

Dietary Fiber: 10.4 g; **Sugars:** 14.4 g

Cholesterol: 0 mg; **Sodium:** 388 mg; **Potassium:** 751 mg;

Vitamin A: 223%; **Vitamin C:** 397%; **Calcium:** 12%; **Iron:** 25%

Ingredients:
Ingredients for the morning:
- ☐ 1/3 cup dry black-eyed peas
- ☐ 1/3 cup carrots, chopped
- ☐ 2 tablespoons bell pepper, minced
- ☐ 2 cups water
- ☐ 1/8-1/4 teaspoon liquid smoke, to taste
- ☐ 1/6 cup millet
- ☐ 1 teaspoon Cajun seasoning
- ☐ 1 clove garlic, minced

Ingredients for the evening:
- ☐ 1 cup mixed leafy greens, minced (kale, collard, etc.)
- ☐ 2 tablespoons tomato paste
- ☐ 2-3 buns, preferably gluten-free, for serving
- ☐ Salt, to taste
- ☐ White pepper, to taste

Directions:
For the morning ingredients:
1. Put all of the ingredients into the slow cooker.
2. Cover and cook for 7-9 hours on LOW.

For the evening ingredients:
1. About 30 minutes before serving time, add the tomato paste and the greens.
2. Cover and continue cooking for 30 minutes.
3. Pile the sloppy joe on your bunds. Enjoy!

Black Bean, Corn, Radish, Lettuce, Cucumber, Grape Tomato, and Spinach Enchiladas

Prep Time: 30 minutes; **Cook Time:** 2 1/2-3 hours on LOW	

Prep Time: 30 minutes; **Cook Time:** 2 1/2-3 hours on LOW

Serving Size: 705 g; **Serves:** 4; **Calories:** 905

Total Fat: 30.1 g **Saturated Fat:** 13.8 g; **Trans Fat:** 0 g

Protein: 48.4 g; **Total Carbs:** 120.8 g

Dietary Fiber: 27.2 g; **Sugars:** 13.9 g

Cholesterol: 60 mg; **Sodium:** 1811 mg; **Potassium:** 3208 mg;

Vitamin A: 163%; **Vitamin C:** 64%; **Calcium:** 73%; **Iron:** 73%

Ingredients:

- ☐ 1 can (15.5-ounce) black beans, rinsed
- ☐ 1 cup frozen corn
- ☐ 1 package (10-ounce) frozen chopped spinach, thawed and squeezed of excess liquid
- ☐ 2 jars (16-ounce each) salsa (3 1/2 cups)
- ☐ 4 radishes, cut into matchsticks
- ☐ 8 ounces vegan cheddar cheese, grated (about 2 cups)
- ☐ 1 romaine lettuce, medium head, chopped (6 cups)
- ☐ 1/2 cucumber, halved and sliced
- ☐ 1/2 cup grape tomatoes, halved
- ☐ 1/2 teaspoon ground cumin
- ☐ 2 tablespoons olive oil
- ☐ 3 tablespoons fresh squeezed lime juice
- ☐ 8 pieces 6-inch corn tortillas, warmed
- ☐ Kosher salt and black pepper
- ☐ Scallions, sliced, for serving

Directions:

1. In a medium-sized bowl, mash 1/2 of the beans. Add the corn, spinach, 1 cup vegan cheddar, cumin, remaining beans, 1/4 teaspoon pepper, and 1/2 teaspoon salt. Stir to combine. Set aside.
2. Spread 1 jar of salsa into the bottom of a 4 to 6-quart slow cooker. Evenly dividing, roll up the bean mixture in the tortillas, about 1/2 cup each tortilla. With the seam-side faced down, put the tortilla wraps in the slow cooker. Top with the remaining salsa and the vegan cheddar.

3. Cover and cook for 2 1/2-3 hours on LOW or until heated through.
4. Before serving, toss the lettuce with the radishes, cucumber, tomatoes, lime juice, 1/2 teaspoon pepper, and 1/2 teaspoon salt in a large-sized bowl.
5. Serve the enchiladas with the lettuce mix and sprinkle with scallions.

Chinese-Style Barbecued Tofu with Vegetables

Prep Time: 30 minutes; **Cook Time:** 4 hours on HIGH

Serving Size: 551 g; **Serves:** 3-4; **Calories:** 360

Total Fat: 8 g **Saturated Fat**: 1.6 g; **Trans Fat**: 0 g

Protein: 18.8 g; **Total Carbs:** 58.5 g

Dietary Fiber: 6.1 g; **Sugars:** 18.2 g

Cholesterol: 1 mg; **Sodium:** 1241 mg; **Potassium:** 1302 mg;

Vitamin A: 26%; **Vitamin C:** 155%; **Calcium:** 39%; **Iron:** 32%

Ingredients:

- ☐ 1 package (about 1 pound) tofu, regular or extra-firm (not silken)
- ☐ 1 can (8-ounce) sliced water chestnuts
- ☐ 1/2 green or red bell pepper, large-sized, cut into 1-inch squares
- ☐ 2 zucchinis, medium-sized, cut into 1/2-inch cubes
- ☐ 2-3 stalks broccoli (stalks only, florets reserved for another use)

For the sauce:
- ☐ 8 ounces tomato sauce, no salt added
- ☐ 3 cloves garlic, minced
- ☐ 2 teaspoons molasses
- ☐ 2 teaspoons fresh ginger, minced
- ☐ 2 tablespoons water
- ☐ 2 tablespoons seasoned rice wine vinegar
- ☐ 1/8 teaspoon ground black pepper
- ☐ 1/4 teaspoon vegan Worcestershire sauce
- ☐ 1/4 teaspoon five-spice powder
- ☐ 1/4 teaspoon crushed red pepper
- ☐ 1/4 cup hoisin sauce
- ☐ 1 tablespoon spicy brown mustard
- ☐ 1 tablespoon soy sauce, low sodium
- ☐ 1 onion, small-sized, minced
- ☐ Salt, to taste, optional

Directions:

1. Cut the tofu into 1/2-inch thick slices. Put them into a couple of pieces of paper towels and then cover them with

2-3 pieces more paper towels. Lightly press to squeeze out some of the moisture. Cut the slices into triangle shapes or other shapes.

2. Put oil into a nonstick skillet and heat until heat. When hot, cook the tofu in the skillet until both sides are well browned.

3. Grease the bowl of the slow cooker. Transfer the tofu into the greased cooker. Set to HIGH and cover.

4. In the same skillet, sauté the ginger, garlic, and onions for 3 minutes or until the onions are soft. Add the rest of the sauce ingredients into the skillet. Stir and heat until bubbly. Pour the sauce mix into over the tofu in the cooker. Stir until well combined. Cover and cook for 3 hours on HIGH.

5. Trim the tough ends off the broccoli stalks. Peel off the outer skin and then slice into 1/4-inch thick rounds.

6. When the tofu is cooked after 3 hours, add the broccoli rounds and the other vegetables into the slow cooker. Stir until well combined. Cover tightly. Cook for 1 additional hour on HIGH or until the veggies are tender but not overcooked.

7. Serve over brown rice.

Notes: If you want to cook the tofu for a longer time, add 2-3 more tablespoons of water into the sauce and cook for 5-6 hours on HIGH before adding the vegetables.

Veggie Fajitas

Prep Time: 10 minutes; **Cook Time:** 3 hours, 30 minutes

Serving Size: 200 g; **Serves:** 2; **Calories:** 186

Total Fat: 8.4 g **Saturated Fat:** 1.1 g; **Trans Fat:** 0 g

Protein: 3.9 g; **Total Carbs:** 26.5 g

Dietary Fiber: 5.5 g; **Sugars:** 5.5 g

Cholesterol: 0 mg; **Sodium:** 37 mg; **Potassium:** 436 mg;

Vitamin A: 36%; **Vitamin C:** 32%; **Calcium:** 6%; **Iron:** 7%

Ingredients:

- ☐ 200 grams cherry tomatoes, halved
- ☐ 3 peppers, cut into strips (I used one green, one red, and one yellow)
- ☐ 1/2 teaspoon ground coriander
- ☐ 1 teaspoon smoked paprika
- ☐ 1 teaspoon hot chili powder
- ☐ 1 tablespoon oil
- ☐ 1 onion, halved and thinly sliced
- ☐ 6 mini flour tortillas, for serving

Toppings:
- ☐ Fresh coriander
- ☐ Cashew Sour cream
- ☐ Salsa
- ☐ Avocado

Directions:

1. Put the onion, peppers, oil, chili powder, paprika, and coriander into the slow cooker. Stir to combine.
2. Cover and cook for 1 1/2 hours on HIGH. Add the tomatoes and cook for 2 hours more.
3. Serve the tortillas with your favorite toppings.

Grains and Lentils

Lentils and Sweet Potato

Prep Time: 15 minutes; **Cook Time:** 4 1/2 hours on HIGH		

Prep Time: 15 minutes; **Cook Time:** 4 1/2 hours on HIGH

Serving Size: 446 g; **Serves:** 6-8; **Calories:** 531

Total Fat: 17.4 g **Saturated Fat:** 14.3 g; **Trans Fat:** 0 g

Protein: 19.1 g; **Total Carbs:** 77.6 g

Dietary Fiber: 23 g; **Sugars:** 5.1 g

Cholesterol: 0 mg; **Sodium:** 614 mg; **Potassium:** 2012 mg;

Vitamin A: 10%; **Vitamin C:** 54%; **Calcium:** 8%; **Iron:** 33%

Ingredients:
- ☐ 1 1/2 cups red lentils, uncooked (masoor dal)
- ☐ 1 can (14 ounces) coconut milk
- ☐ 3 sweet potatoes, large-sized, diced (about 6 cups)
- ☐ 1 cup water
- ☐ 1 onion, minced
- ☐ 1/2 teaspoon salt
- ☐ 2 teaspoons chili powder
- ☐ 2 teaspoons garam masala
- ☐ 2 teaspoons ground coriander
- ☐ 3 cups vegetable broth
- ☐ 4 cloves garlic, minced

Directions:
1. Put the sweet potatoes, garlic, onion, spices, and vegetable broth into the slow cooker.
2. Cover and cook for 3 hours on HIGH or until the vegetables are soft.
3. Add the lentils and stir once to combine. Cover and cook for 1 1/2 hours on HIGH.
4. Stir in the coconut milk and then add as much water as needed for the dish to reach your desired consistency.

Quinoa with Corn, Chickpeas, and Black Beans

Prep Time: 5 minutes; **Cook Time:** 3-4 hours on HIGH	

Prep Time: 5 minutes; **Cook Time:** 3-4 hours on HIGH

Serving Size: 339 g; **Serves:** 4; **Calories:** 449

Total Fat: 6.5 g **Saturated Fat**: 0.9 g; **Trans Fat**: 0 g

Protein: 22.6 g; **Total Carbs:** 78.4 g

Dietary Fiber: 14.9 g; **Sugars:** 10.1 g

Cholesterol: 0 mg; **Sodium:** 673 mg; **Potassium:** 1300 mg;

Vitamin A: 21%; **Vitamin C:** 129%; **Calcium:** 11%; **Iron:** 46%

Ingredients:

- ☐ 1 cup frozen corn
- ☐ 1 cup quinoa, uncooked
- ☐ 2/3 cup chickpeas, reduced sodium, drained and rinsed
- ☐ 1/2 cup black beans, drained and rinsed
- ☐ 1 cup red pepper, chopped, about 1 large pepper
- ☐ 1 cup Roma tomato, chopped (about 2 tomatoes)
- ☐ 1 tablespoon garlic, minced
- ☐ 1 to 1 1/2 tablespoons adobo sauce from canned chipotle peppers
- ☐ 1/2 cup onion, roughly chopped, about 1/2 large onion
- ☐ 1/2 tablespoon cumin
- ☐ 1/4 teaspoon salt
- ☐ 2 cups vegetable broth, reduced sodium
- ☐ Fresh cilantro, for garnish
- ☐ Pinch black pepper
- ☐ Vegan cheddar cheese, shredded, for garnish

Directions:

1. Grease the slow cooker with nonstick cooking spray. Except for the vegan cheese and the and cilantro, put all the ingredients into the slow cooker.
2. Cover and cook for 3-4 hours on HIGH. Check after 3 hours into cooking time to make sure the quinoa is not burning.
3. When cooking time is up, taste and, if needed, season with more salt and pepper to taste. Garnish with the cheese and cilantro.

Notes: This dish is spicy. If you want a less spicy dish, just reduce the adobo sauce to 1 tablespoon.

Indian Spiced Lentils

Prep Time: 10 minutes; **Cook Time:** 3 hours on HIGH

Serving Size: 360 g; **Serves:** 4; **Calories:** 517

Total Fat: 2.4 g **Saturated Fat:** 0 g; **Trans Fat:** 0 g

Protein: 35 g; **Total Carbs:** 91.2 g

Dietary Fiber: 40.9 g; **Sugars:** 11.9 g

Cholesterol: 0 mg; **Sodium:** 709 mg; **Potassium:** 1846 mg;

Vitamin A: 43%; **Vitamin C:** 144%; **Calcium:** 11%; **Iron:** 71%

Ingredients:

- ☐ 2 1/2 cups lentils, cooked
- ☐ 1 can (15 ounces) tomato sauce
- ☐ 1 sweet potato, peeled and finely diced
- ☐ 1 lemon, juices
- ☐ 1 onion, medium-sized, finely diced
- ☐ 1 tablespoons ground coriander
- ☐ 1 teaspoon garam masala
- ☐ 1 teaspoon ground turmeric
- ☐ 1 yellow bell pepper, finely diced
- ☐ 1/2 teaspoon ground ginger
- ☐ 1/4 teaspoon cayenne, or more to taste
- ☐ 2 teaspoons ground cumin
- ☐ 2 teaspoons paprika
- ☐ 2/3 cup vegetable broth, organic
- ☐ 3-4 cloves garlic, finely diced
- ☐ Salt and pepper, to taste

Directions:

1. Put all the ingredients into the slow cooker. Cook for 3 hours on HIGH or until the sweet potatoes are cooked and soft.
2. Serve with naan bread and cooked brown rice.

Chickpea, Lentil, and Sweet Potato Coconut Curry

Prep Time: 10 minutes; **Cook Time:** 4 hours on HIGH; 8 hours on LOW

Serving Size: 435 g; **Serves:** 7; **Calories:** 629	
Total Fat: 12.2 g **Saturated Fat:** 4 g; **Trans Fat:** 0 g	
Protein: 36.1 g; **Total Carbs:** 98.1 g	
Dietary Fiber: 30.8 g; **Sugars:** 15.3 g	
Cholesterol: 0 mg; **Sodium**: 874 mg; **Potassium**: 1620 mg;	
Vitamin A: 3%; **Vitamin C:** 19%; **Calcium:** 16%; **Iron:** 65%	

Ingredients:

- ☐ 1 can (15 ounces) lite coconut milk
- ☐ 1 cup dry lentils, picked over and rinsed
- ☐ 2 cans (15 ounces each) chickpeas (a.k.a. garbanzo beans), drained and rinsed
- ☐ 1 sweet potato, large-sized, cut into small cubes
- ☐ 1 teaspoon ground ginger
- ☐ 1 teaspoon ground turmeric
- ☐ 1/2 teaspoon salt
- ☐ 1/4 teaspoon pepper
- ☐ 2 tablespoons curry powder (I used mild curry)
- ☐ 6 cups vegetable broth

Directions:

1. Put all of the ingredients in the slow cooker. Stir and mix well.
2. Cover and cook for 4 hours on HIGH or for 8 hours on LOW.
3. Taste and, if needed, season with salt and pepper.

Black Bean, Refried Beans, Quinoa Stuffed Peppers

Prep Time: 15 minutes; **Cook Time:** 6 hours on LOW; 3 hours on HIGH

Serving Size: 350 g; **Serves:** 6; **Calories:** 569

Total Fat: 14.2 g **Saturated Fat:** 6.7 g; **Trans Fat:** 0 g

Protein: 30.5 g; **Total Carbs:** 82.7 g

Dietary Fiber: 17.8 g; **Sugars:** 8.6 g

Cholesterol: 35 mg; **Sodium:** 781 mg; **Potassium:** 1590 mg;

Vitamin A: 115%; **Vitamin C:** 396%; **Calcium:** 34%; **Iron:** 38%

Ingredients:
- ☐ 6 bell peppers
- ☐ 1 1/2 cups red enchilada sauce
- ☐ 1 1/2 cups vegan pepper jack cashew cheese, shredded
- ☐ 1 can (14 ounces) black beans, rinsed and drained
- ☐ 1 can (14 ounces) refried beans
- ☐ 1 cup quinoa, uncooked, rinsed
- ☐ 1 teaspoon chili powder
- ☐ 1 teaspoon cumin
- ☐ 1 teaspoon onion powder
- ☐ 1/2 teaspoon garlic salt
- ☐ Avocado, cilantro, cashew sour cream, etc., for topping

Directions:
1. Cut the pepper tops off. Scrape out the seeds and the ribs.
2. In a large-sized bowl, combine the beans with the quinoa, spices, enchilada sauce, and 1 cup of the vegan cheese. Fill each pepper with the bean mix.
3. Pour 1/2 cup of water into the slow cooker. Put the stuffed peppers in the slow cooker. Cover and cook for 6 hours on LOW or for 3 hours on HIGH.
4. Uncover and sprinkle the remaining 1/2 cup vegan cheese between each pepper top.
5. Cover and let sit for a couple minutes or until the cheese is melted.
6. Serve with your prepared pairing. They are great with guacamole and chips.

Lentil-Butternut Squash Curry

Prep Time: 30 minutes; **Cook Time:** 6-8 hours on LOW

Serving Size: 209 g; **Serves:** 8; **Calories:** 320

Total Fat: 12.6 g **Saturated Fat:** 10.6 g; **Trans Fat:** 0 g

Protein: 14.7 g; **Total Carbs:** 40.2 g

Dietary Fiber: 17.8 g; **Sugars:** 5.8 g

Cholesterol: 0 mg; **Sodium:** 602 mg; **Potassium:** 895 mg;

Vitamin A: 109%; **Vitamin C:** 33%; **Calcium:** 7%; **Iron:** 28%

Ingredients:
- ☐ 2 cups butternut squash, diced
- ☐ 2 cups red or brown lentils
- ☐ 14-ounce canned coconut milk
- ☐ 15-ounce canned diced tomatoes
- ☐ 1 carrot, large-sized, sliced
- ☐ 1 onion, diced
- ☐ 1 tablespoon curry powder
- ☐ 2 teaspoons salt
- ☐ 4 cups water

Directions:
1. Put all the ingredients in the slow cooker and then stir to combine.
2. Cover and cook for 6 to 8 hours on LOW. Check halfway through cooking time. If needed, add more water.
3. Serve with flatbread, hot cooked rice, or raita.

Quinoa with Carrot, Green Beans, and Sweet Pepper

Prep Time: 10 minutes; **Cook Time:** 4-6 hours on LOW; 2-4 hours on HIGH

Serving Size: 335 g; **Serves:** 4; **Calories:** 313

Total Fat: 7.7 g **Saturated Fat:** 1 g; **Trans Fat:** 0 g

Protein: 11 g; **Total Carbs:** 51.3 g

Dietary Fiber: 7.7 g; **Sugars:** 5 g

Cholesterol: 0 mg; **Sodium:** 103 mg; **Potassium:** 569 mg;

Vitamin A: 75%; **Vitamin C:** 109%; **Calcium:** 6%; **Iron:** 19%

Ingredients:
- ☐ 1 1/2 cups quinoa
- ☐ 1 carrot, small-sized, chopped
- ☐ 1 cup fresh green beans, chopped
- ☐ 1 onion, small-sized, chopped
- ☐ 1 sweet red pepper, medium-sized, chopped
- ☐ 1 tablespoon olive oil
- ☐ 1/4 teaspoon pepper
- ☐ 2 garlic cloves, minced
- ☐ 3 cups vegetable stock
- ☐ 1 teaspoon fresh cilantro or basil (depending on your taste), for serving

Directions:
1. Rinse the quinoa. Put into a 6-quart crockpot. Add 1 tablespoon of olive oil and toss to coat. Stir in the vegetables, garlic, pepper, and broth.
2. Cover and cook for 4 to 6 hours on LOW or for 2 to 4 hours on HIGH.
3. The quinoa is cooked with it is tender and can be fluffed using a fork.
4. Top with fresh cilantro. Serve.

You can add black beans or garbanzo beans into the dish to add protein and make it into a complete meal.

Vegan Sausage, Seitan, Tomato, and Rice Jambalaya

Prep Time: 25 minutes; **Cook Time:** 4 hours on LOW, plus 30 minutes on HIGH

Serving Size: 408 g; **Serves:** 6; **Calories:** 458	
Total Fat: 15.7 g **Saturated Fat:** 4.6 g; **Trans Fat:** 0 g	
Protein: 40.6 g; **Total Carbs:** 33.1 g	
Dietary Fiber: 4.3 g; **Sugars:** 4.8 g	
Cholesterol: 32 mg; **Sodium:** 1145 mg; **Potassium:** 565 mg;	
Vitamin A: 31%; **Vitamin C:** 66%; **Calcium:** 4%; **Iron:** 15%	

Ingredients:
- ☐ 8 ounces smoked vegan sausage, cut into 2-inch slices
- ☐ 8 ounces seitan, cut into cubes
- ☐ 1 can (28 ounce) diced tomatoes with its juice
- ☐ 1 cup rice
- ☐ 3 stalks celery, chopped
- ☐ 2 cloves garlic, minced
- ☐ 1/2 teaspoon dried thyme
- ☐ 1/2 teaspoon dried oregano
- ☐ 1/2 onion, large-sized, chopped
- ☐ 1/2 green bell pepper, large-sized, seeded and chopped
- ☐ 1 tablespoon olive oil, or to taste
- ☐ 1 tablespoon miso paste
- ☐ 1 tablespoon fresh parsley, chopped, or to taste, optional
- ☐ 1 cup vegetable broth
- ☐ 1 1/2 teaspoons Cajun seasoning

Directions:
1. Grease the bottom of a 4-quart slow cooker with olive oil.
2. Except for the rice, put all the ingredients in the slow cooker and stir to combine.
3. Cover and cook for 4 hours on LOW.
4. After 4 hours, add the rice into the cooker. Set the cooker to HIGH and cook for 30 minutes or until the rice is cooked. Garnish with parsley and serve.

Black-Eyed Pea, Sweet Corn, Tomato, and Rice Southwest Dinner

Prep Time: 20 minutes; **Cook Time:** 2 hours on HIGH

Serving Size: 472 g; **Serves:** 6; **Calories:** 585

Total Fat: 8.4 g **Saturated Fat:** 2.8 g; **Trans Fat:** 0 g

Protein: 20.4 g; **Total Carbs:** 117.5 g

Dietary Fiber: 13.9 g; **Sugars:** 14.1 g

Cholesterol: 10 mg; **Sodium:** 174 mg; **Potassium:** 1370 mg;

Vitamin A: 68%; **Vitamin C:** 125%; **Calcium:** 14%; **Iron:** 67%

Ingredients:
- 1 1/2 cups dried black-eyed peas, soaked overnight
- 1 can (10 ounce) sweet corn, drained
- 1 can (28 ounce) diced tomatoes
- 1 green bell pepper, diced
- 1 onion, chopped
- 1/2 cup cashew cheddar cheese
- 1/4 cup chili powder
- 2 cups rice, cooked
- 2 teaspoons ground cumin
- Garlic cloves, chopped

Directions:
1. Drain the black-eyed peas and then rinse thoroughly. Put into the slow cooker.
2. Add the tomatoes, corn, garlic, onion, and green pepper into the cooker. Season with cumin and chili powder and stir well until blended.
3. Cover and cook for 2 hours on HIGH.
4. After cooking time is complete, stir in the rice and cheese.
5. Cook for 30 more minutes.

Mexican Quinoa, Corn, Chickpea, and Black Beans

Prep Time: 5 minutes; **Cook Time:** 3-4 hours on HIGH	

Serving Size: 353 g; **Serves:** 4; **Calories:** 447
Total Fat: 6.4 g **Saturated Fat:** 0.9 g; **Trans Fat:** 0 g
Protein: 22.9 g; **Total Carbs:** 77.6 g
Dietary Fiber: 15.1 g; **Sugars:** 9.5 g
Cholesterol: 0 mg; **Sodium:** 778 mg; **Potassium:** 1351 mg;
Vitamin A: 31%; **Vitamin C:** 119%; **Calcium:** 11%; **Iron:** 41%

Ingredients:

- ☐ 2/3 cup chickpeas, reduced sodium, drained and rinsed
- ☐ 1/2 cup black beans, drained and rinsed
- ☐ 1 cup frozen corn
- ☐ 1 cup quinoa, uncooked
- ☐ 1 cup red pepper, chopped, about 1 large pepper
- ☐ 1 cup Roma tomato, chopped (about 2 tomatoes)
- ☐ 1 tablespoon garlic, minced
- ☐ 1/2 cup onion, roughly chopped, about 1/2 large onion
- ☐ 1/2 tablespoon cumin
- ☐ 1/4 teaspoon salt
- ☐ 1- 1 1/2 tablespoons adobo sauce from 1 can chipotle peppers in adobo sauce
- ☐ cups vegetable broth, reduced sodium
- ☐ Fresh cilantro, for garnish
- ☐ Vegan cheese, for garnish
- ☐ Pinch black pepper

Directions:

1. Grease the slow cooker with nonstick cooking spray. Put the all the ingredients in the greased cooker and stir well to combine.
2. Cook for 3 to 4 hours on HIGH. Check after 3 hours into cooking time.
3. When cooked, taste and, if needed, season with salt and pepper to taste. Garnish each serving with cilantro and cheese.

Notes: This dish is a bit spicy. If you like a tamer spiciness, use 1 tablespoon of adobo sauce instead.

Vegan Red Beans and Rice

Prep Time: 20 minutes; **Cook Time:** 6-8 hours on HIGH	
Serving Size: 112 g; **Serves:** 8; **Calories:** 215	
Total Fat: 0.8 g **Saturated Fat:** 0 g; **Trans Fat:** 0 g	
Protein: 13.6 g; **Total Carbs:** 40.1 g	
Dietary Fiber: 9.9 g; **Sugars:** 3.5 g	
Cholesterol: 0 mg; **Sodium:** 43 mg; **Potassium:** 911 mg;	
Vitamin A: 17%; **Vitamin C:** 114%; **Calcium:** 7%; **Iron:** 26%	

Ingredients:
- 1 pound dry red kidney beans
- 5 stalks celery, diced finely (about 1 1/2 cups)
- 1 green bell pepper, large-sized, diced finely (about 1 1/2 cups)
- 1 onion, large-sized, diced finely (about 1 1/2 cups)
- 1 teaspoon Liquid Smoke
- 1/2 tablespoon red pepper sauce (such as Tabasco)
- 1/2 teaspoon black pepper
- 1/4-1 teaspoon red pepper
- 2 chipotle peppers in adobo sauce, chopped
- 2 teaspoons oregano
- 2 teaspoons thyme
- 3 bay leaves
- 5 cloves garlic, minced
- Rice, cooked, for serving
- Salt, to taste

Directions:
1. Soak the beans overnight in water. Drain and rinse. Put in the slow cooker. Pour enough to cover the beans with 1 inch of water.
2. Except for the rice and salt, add the rest of the ingredients into the slow cooker.
3. Cover and cook for 6-8 hours on HIGH or until the beans are soft.
4. Just before serving, season with salt and then mash up using a potato masher.
5. Serve over hot cooked rice.

Greek Rice with Kalamata Olives, Bell Pepper, and Vegan Feta

Prep Time: 20 minutes; **Cook Time:** 1 1/2 hours on HIGH

Serving Size: 332 g; **Serves**: 6-8; **Calories:** 404

Total Fat: 13.6 g **Saturated Fat:** 6.4 g; **Trans Fat**: 0 g

Protein: 11.3 g; **Total Carbs:** 59 g

Dietary Fiber: 3.2 g; **Sugars:** 5.5 g

Cholesterol: 33 mg; **Sodium**: 664 mg; **Potassium**: 225 mg;

Vitamin A: 32%; **Vitamin C:** 134%; **Calcium:** 23%; **Iron**: 22%

Ingredients:

- ☐ 2 cups rice (I used Uncle Ben's Converted)
- ☐ 3/4 cup Kalamata olives, sliced (or regular black olives)
- ☐ 1 cup vegan feta cheese, crumbled (I used Soy Feta) PLUS 1/2 cup more, for sprinkling, if desired
- ☐ 1 green bell pepper, seeded and finely chopped
- ☐ 1 onion, chopped small
- ☐ 1 red bell pepper, seeded and finely chopped
- ☐ 1 tablespoon garlic, minced
- ☐ 1 tablespoon PLUS 1 teaspoon olive oil
- ☐ 1 teaspoon dried oregano (preferably Greek oregano)
- ☐ 1 teaspoon Greek Seasoning
- ☐ 1/4 cup green onion, sliced (or more, to taste)
- ☐ 1-2 tablespoons fresh squeezed lemon juice
- ☐ 2 cans (14 ounces each) vegetable stock PLUS enough water to make 4 cups
- ☐ Salt and fresh ground black pepper, to taste

Directions:

1. In a large-sized frying pan, heat 1 tablespoon of olive oil. Add the rice. Sauté until the rice is nicely browned, but not burnt – carefully watch. Transfer the rice into the cooker.
2. Add the 1 teaspoon olive oil into the same pan. Add the onions; cook for about 4 to 5 minutes or until they start to brown.
3. Add the garlic, dried oregano, and Greek seasoning; cook for a few minutes more.

4. Add the stock or water mix. Deglaze the pan, scraping off any browned bits from the bottom. Put the stock mix into the slow cooker.
5. Cover and cook for 1 1/2 hours on HIGH.
6. While the rice is cooking, prepare the green onions, bell peppers, and feta.
7. When the cooking time is done and the rice is fairly soft, but still not completely cooked, add the bell peppers; cook for 15 minutes. Add the feta and olives; cook for 15 minutes.
8. Check if the rice is cooked to your preferred doneness. Stir in the lemon juice and then season to taste with salt and pepper. Top with the additional feta and garnish with the green onions. Serve hot.

Brown Rice and Black Beans Mexican Bowl with Avocado-Poblano Salsa

Prep Time: 30 minutes; **Cook Time:** 1 1/2 hours on HIGH, plus 30 minutes on HIGH

Serving Size: 403 g; **Serves:** 6; **Calories:** 812	
Total Fat: 15.9 g **Saturated Fat:** 3 g; **Trans Fat:** 0 g	
Protein: 38.4 g; **Total Carbs:** 136.3 g	
Dietary Fiber: 31.8 g; **Sugars:** 15.1 g	
Cholesterol: 0 mg; **Sodium:** 342 mg; **Potassium:** 2977 mg;	
Vitamin A: 135%; **Vitamin C:** 186%; **Calcium:** 22%; **Iron:** 55%	

Ingredients:

For the slow cooker:

- 1 can (4 ounce) diced green Anaheim chilies plus juice
- 1 cup brown rice, long-grain (I used Uncle Ben's Brown Rice)
- 1 cup onion, finely chopped
- 1 green bell pepper, chopped small
- 1 red bell pepper, chopped small
- 2 cans (15 ounces each) black beans, rinsed well and drained
- 2 cups vegetable stock (I used 1 vegetable broth plus water to make 2 cups)
- Salt, to taste

For the salsa:

- 1 avocado, large-sized (or 2 small-sized avocadoes), cut into 1 inch cubes
- 1 Poblano pepper, large-sized, very finely diced
- 1 tablespoon PLUS 2 tablespoons lime juice (fresh-squeezed or fresh-frozen)
- 1/2 cup fresh cilantro, finely chopped
- 1/2 cup green onion, thinly sliced
- 1/2 cup tomato, diced
- 1/2 teaspoon ground cumin, or more to taste
- 2 tablespoons olive oil, extra-virgin
- Salt, to taste

Directions:

1. Put the rice, broth, and onion into a 3-quart slow cooker. Stir to combine.
2. Cover and cook for 1 1/2 hours on HIGH or until the rice is beginning to tender.
3. Meanwhile, prepare the bell peppers, green chilies, and black beans.
4. After 1 1/2 hours, add the bell peppers, green chilies, and black beans in the cooker. Gently stir to combine with the rice and season with salt to taste. Cover and cook for 30 minutes more on HIGH.
5. Meanwhile, prepare the salsa ingredients. In a large-sized bowl that can hold all the salsa ingredients, toss the avocado with 1 tablespoon of lime juice. Add the remaining salsa ingredients into the bowl and gently combine.
6. The rice mixture is done when the rice is tender and the peppers are cooked with a little bit of crunch in them.
7. Serve the rice mix hot or warm. Top each serving with a generous scoop of the salsa. You can add any of your choice toppings.

Red Lentil, Cauliflower, Cilantro, and Spinach Curry

Prep Time: 10 minutes; **Cook Time:** 6-8 hours on LOW

Serving Size: 307 g; **Serves:** 8; **Calories:** 251

Total Fat: 3.7 g **Saturated Fat**: 0 g; **Trans Fat**: 0 g

Protein: 17.3 g; **Total Carbs:** 38.1 g

Dietary Fiber: 17.1 g; **Sugars:** 5.1 g

Cholesterol: 0 mg; **Sodium:** 715 mg; **Potassium**: 998 mg;

Vitamin A: 77%; **Vitamin C:** 55%; **Calcium**: 9%; **Iron**: 29%

Ingredients:
- 2 cups frozen cauliflower
- 2 cups red lentils
- 10 ounces fresh spinach (can substitute frozen, if needed)
- 1 can (15 ounce) diced tomatoes
- 1/4 cup cilantro, chopped
- 1 onion, chopped
- 1 tablespoon lime juice
- 1 tablespoon minced garlic
- 1 teaspoon ground ginger
- 1/2 teaspoon cayenne pepper
- 1/2 teaspoon ground coriander
- 1/2 teaspoon ground cumin
- 1-1/2 teaspoons salt
- 2 tablespoons curry paste (I used mild)
- 2 teaspoons sugar
- 4 cups vegetable broth

Directions:
1. Except for the cilantro and lime juice, combine all of the ingredients into the slow cooker.
2. Cover and cook for 6-8 hours on LOW.
3. When the cooking time is up, stir in the cilantro and the lime juice. Serve.

Pumpkin, Red Lentil, and Chickpea Curry

Prep Time: 10 minutes; **Cook Time:** 8 to 10 hours on LOW; 5 to 6 hours on HIGH

Serving Size: 580 g; **Serves:** 4-6; **Calories:** 1247	

Serving Size: 580 g; **Serves:** 4-6; **Calories:** 1247

Total Fat: 39.8 g **Saturated Fat:** 24.2 g; **Trans Fat:** 0 g

Protein: 59.6 g; **Total Carbs:** 173.1 g

Dietary Fiber: 56.9 g; **Sugars:** 30.9 g

Cholesterol: 195 mg; **Sodium:** 1038 mg; **Potassium:** 2901 mg;

Vitamin A: 0%; **Vitamin C:** 31%; **Calcium:** 30%; **Iron:** 113%

Ingredients:
- ☐ 2 cans (15-ounce each) chickpeas, drained
- ☐ 1 can (15-ounce) coconut milk, full fat
- ☐ 1 cup pumpkin puree
- ☐ 1 cup red lentils, rinsed
- ☐ 1 tablespoon curry powder
- ☐ 1 teaspoon kosher salt, or more to taste
- ☐ 1 yellow onion, medium-sized, diced
- ☐ 1/4 teaspoon ground cayenne pepper
- ☐ 2 cloves garlic, medium-sized, minced
- ☐ 2 cups vegetable broth, low-sodium

For serving:
- ☐ Brown rice, white rice, or cauliflower rice
- ☐ Cilantro leaves
- ☐ Fresh sliced lime wedges

Directions:
1. Except for the coconut milk, put all of the ingredients into a 3 quart or larger-sized slow cooker.
2. Cover and cook for 8 to 10 hours on LOW or for 5 to 6 hours on HIGH.
3. After the cooking time is up, stir in the coconut milk.
4. Cover and cook for another 30 minutes on LOW. The curry will be thin at first. It will thicken as it sits.
5. Spoon the curry over cooked rice. Serve with fresh-sliced lime wedges and cilantro.

Red Lentil Dal

Prep Time: 10 minutes; **Cook Time:** 4-5 hours on HIGH; for 8-10 hours on LOW

Serving Size: 296 g; **Serves:** 10-12; **Calories:** 238

Total Fat: 1.3 g **Saturated Fat**: 0 g; **Trans Fat**: 0 g

Protein: 16.3 g; **Total Carbs:** 41.3 g

Dietary Fiber: 19.5 g; **Sugars:** 3.8 g

Cholesterol: 0 mg; **Sodium:** 202 mg; **Potassium:** 814 mg;

Vitamin A: 14%; **Vitamin C**: 25%; **Calcium**: 6%; **Iron**: 32%

Ingredients:

- ☐ 3 cups red lentils (you can use a mix of split mung beans or yellow split peas, or a combination of two or more)
- ☐ 1 can (28 ounces) diced tomatoes
- ☐ 1 bay leaf
- ☐ 1 onion, larges-sized, diced
- ☐ 1 tablespoon turmeric
- ☐ 1 teaspoon fennel seeds
- ☐ 1 teaspoon sea salt
- ☐ 1/4 teaspoon black pepper, fresh ground
- ☐ 2 tablespoons fresh grated ginger
- ☐ 2 teaspoons cumin seeds
- ☐ 2 teaspoons fenugreek seeds
- ☐ 2 teaspoons mustard seeds
- ☐ 2 teaspoons onion seeds or nigella
- ☐ 3 green cardamom pods
- ☐ 4 garlic cloves, minced
- ☐ 6 cups water

For serving:
- ☐ Brown rice, hot cooked
- ☐ Cilantro, optional
- ☐ Extra cumin seeds and onion, optional
- ☐ Lemon juice, fresh squeezed, optional

Directions:

1. Put the split peas and the lentils into a large-sized bowl. Pour enough water to cover and let soak for a couple of

minutes. Swish and wash the peas and lentils. Drain well and rinse.

2. Pour 6 cups of water into the slow cooker. Add the tomatoes, garlic, onion, turmeric, ginger, bay leaf, cardamom pods, black pepper, and salt. Stir to combine.

3. Over medium heat, heat a small-sized skillet. Put all the seeds into the pan. Shake the pan and stir the seeds using a wooden spoon while toasting until fragrant. Remove from the heat and transfer into the slow cooker. Stir until well combined.

4. Cover and cook for 4 to5 hours on HIGH or for 8-10 hours on LOW. Uncover and stir. Taste and if the lentils are still not soft, cook for about 30 to 60 minutes more. If needed, season with more salt and pepper.

5. To serve, ladle the dal over cooked browned rice. Top each serving with fresh-squeezed lemon, more seeds, and cilantro.

Lentil, Pea, Potato, and Carrot Shepherd's Pie

Prep Time: 10 minutes; **Cook Time:** 6 hours on LOW; 3 hours on HIGH		

Serving Size: 376 g; **Serves:** 6; **Calories:** 373		
Total Fat: 3.7 g **Saturated Fat:** 0.6 g; **Trans Fat:** 0 g		
Protein: 18 g; **Total Carbs:** 68 g		
Dietary Fiber: 22.2 g; **Sugars:** 6.6 g		
Cholesterol: 0 mg; **Sodium:** 700 mg; **Potassium:** 1659 mg;		
Vitamin A: 94%; **Vitamin C:** 57%; **Calcium:** 8%; **Iron:** 29%		

Ingredients:

- ☐ 1 1/2 cups puy lentils, picked over and then rinsed well
- ☐ 1 can (400 grams) diced tomatoes
- ☐ 1 cup frozen peas
- ☐ 4 cups potatoes, mashed OR sweet potatoes, baked, for serving
- ☐ 2 carrots, large-sized, peeled and diced
- ☐ 1 tablespoon olive oil, extra-virgin
- ☐ 1 teaspoon salt
- ☐ 1 yellow onion, large-sized, diced
- ☐ 1/2 teaspoon black pepper, fresh cracked
- ☐ 1/2 teaspoon dried thyme
- ☐ 2 cloves garlic, crushed
- ☐ 2 cups vegetable broth
- ☐ 4 stalks celery, diced

Directions:

1. Except for the peas and mashed potatoes, combine the rest of the ingredients into the slow cooker.
2. Cover and cook for 6 hours on LOW or for 3 hours on HIGH.
3. When the cooking time is up, stir in the peas until combined.
4. Spoon into serving bowls. Top each serving with a scoop of mashed potatoes. Alternatively, you can spoon the lentil mixture into split baked sweet potatoes. You can also spoon the lentil mixture into individual ramekins, and top each with mashed potato and then bake for 20-30

minutes in a 400F or 200C oven until the edges of the filling starts bubbling and the potatoes are golden.

Wild Rice, Mushroom, and Carrot Medley

Prep Time: 0 minutes; **Cook Time:** 0 hours

Serving Size: 90 g; **Serves:** 6-8; **Calories:** 115

Total Fat: 0.4 g **Saturated Fat:** 0 g; **Trans Fat:** 0 g

Protein: 5.3 g; **Total Carbs:** 24.1 g

Dietary Fiber: 2.7 g; **Sugars:** 2.5 g

Cholesterol: 0 mg; **Sodium:** 14 mg; **Potassium:** 285 mg;

Vitamin A: 34%; **Vitamin C:** 5%; **Calcium:** 2%; **Iron:** 8%

Ingredients:

- ☐ 1 carrot, large-sized, diced
- ☐ 1 cup wild rice
- ☐ 2 1/2 cups mushroom or vegetable broth
- ☐ 1 onion, medium-sized, diced
- ☐ 1 stalk celery, diced
- ☐ 1/2 teaspoon dried chervil or dried parsley
- ☐ 2 cloves garlic, minced
- ☐ 2 tablespoons dried porcini
- ☐ Black pepper

Directions:

1. Put all of the ingredients into the slow cooker and stir to combine.
2. Cover and cook for 4 hours on LOW. Uncover and check if the kernels are tender and open. If not, continue cooking until they are, checking every 15 minutes to avoid overcooking.
3. Serve hot.

Madras Lentils and Potatoes

Prep Time: 10 minutes; **Cook Time:** 3 1/2 to 4 hours on HIGH	

Serving Size: 319 g; **Serves:** 4; **Calories:** 557

Total Fat: 17.2 g **Saturated Fat:** 12 g; **Trans Fat:** 0 g

Protein: 28.4 g; **Total Carbs:** 75.7 g

Dietary Fiber: 33.2 g; **Sugars:** 9.1 g

Cholesterol: 23 mg; **Sodium:** 1008 mg; **Potassium:** 1621 mg;

Vitamin A: 15%; **Vitamin C:** 40%; **Calcium:** 10%; **Iron:** 54%

Ingredients:
- ☐ 2 cups lentils, cooked
- ☐ 2 cups canned tomato sauce or puree
- ☐ 1 potato, large-sized, peeled and cubed (1 russet or couple of Yukon gold)
- ☐ 1/2 cup coconut milk, unsweetened
- ☐ 1/2 large-sized onion, finely diced
- ☐ 1/2 teaspoon cumin
- ☐ 1/2 teaspoon dried oregano
- ☐ 1/2 teaspoon kosher salt
- ☐ 3 cloves garlic, minced
- ☐ 3 tablespoons butter
- ☐ Black pepper, fresh ground, to taste
- ☐ Red pepper flakes, to taste

Directions:
1. Put all of the ingredients into the slow cooker.
2. Cover and cook for 3 1/2 to 4 hours on HIGH.
3. When the cooking time is up, taste the dish and, if needed, season to suit your taste. If desired, add an extra pinch of red pepper flakes.
4. Serve over quinoa or rice, along with your favorite big green salad.

Greek-Inspired Stuffed Peppers

Prep Time: 15 minutes; **Cook Time:** 4 hours on HIGH

Serving Size: 283 g; **Serves:** 4; **Calories:** 580

Total Fat: 9.4 g **Saturated Fat:** 5.8 g; **Trans Fat:** 0 g

Protein: 34.7 g; **Total Carbs:** 92.8 g

Dietary Fiber: 29.8 g; **Sugars:** 10.3 g

Cholesterol: 33 mg; **Sodium:** 452 mg; **Potassium:** 1831 mg;

Vitamin A: 86%; **Vitamin C:** 399%; **Calcium:** 37%; **Iron:** 56%

Ingredients:

- [ ] 4 bell peppers, large-sized
- [ ] 1 can (15 ounces) cannellini beans, rinsed and drained
- [ ] 1 cup vegan feta cheese, crumbled (about 4 ounces – I used soy feta)
- [ ] 1 clove garlic, minced
- [ ] 1 teaspoon dried oregano
- [ ] 1/2 cup couscous
- [ ] 4 scallions, green and white parts separated, thinly sliced
- [ ] Coarse salt and freshly ground pepper
- [ ] Lemon wedges, for serving

Directions:

1. Cut a very thin slice from the bottom of each bell pepper to help them sit in the slow cooker. Just below the stems, cut the tops off from the peppers. Discard the stems, chop the tops, and place the chopped tops in a medium-sized bowl. Remove the seeds and ribs from the peppers.
2. Into the bowl with the chopped peppers, add the beans, couscous, feta, garlic, scallion whites, and oregano. Season to taste with salt and pepper and then toss to combine.
3. Fill the peppers with the bean mixture and then place the stuffed peppers into the slow cooker.
4. Cover and cook for 4 hours on HIGH.
5. When the cooking time is up, carefully transfer the stuffed peppers onto a serving plate. Sprinkle each with scallion greens and peppers. Serve with fresh lemon wedges.

Dinner

Coconut, Mushroom, Bok Choy, and Basil Tofu

Prep Time: 5 minutes; **Cook Time:** 4 hours on HIGH

Serving Size: 460 g; **Serves:** 4; **Calories:** 409

Total Fat: 29.3 g **Saturated Fat:** 22.1 g; **Trans Fat:** 0 g

Protein: 17.5 g; **Total Carbs:** 25.3 g

Dietary Fiber: 5.5 g; **Sugars:** 9.4 g

Cholesterol: 0 mg; **Sodium:** 1412 mg; **Potassium:** 954 mg;

Vitamin A: 69%; **Vitamin C:** 65%; **Calcium:** 34%; **Iron:** 36%

Ingredients:
- ☐ 1 package firm tofu, cut into large strips
- ☐ 4 cups baby bok choy, washed and larger pieces cut in half
- ☐ 3/4 onion, mediums-sized, sliced into large chunks
- ☐ 8 ounces mushrooms, sliced
- ☐ 1 can (14 ounces) lite coconut milk
- ☐ 1 cup vegetable broth, low-sodium
- ☐ 2 tablespoons tamari, gluten-free
- ☐ 2 tablespoons rice wine vinegar
- ☐ 1 tablespoons fish sauce
- ☐ 3/4 cup fresh basil, chopped
- ☐ 2 garlic cloves, minced
- ☐ 1 1/2 tablespoons fresh ginger, minced
- ☐ 1/2 teaspoon crushed red pepper flakes
- ☐ 1 tablespoon coconut palm sugar
- ☐ 1/4 cup cornstarch
- ☐ 1/2 teaspoon salt

Directions:
1. Set the slow cooker to HIGH.
2. Add the coconut milk, broth, fish sauce, tamari, wine vinegar, basil, garlic, and ginger into the cooker. Stir to combine.
3. Add the mushrooms, tofu, onion, bok choy, sugar, and red pepper. Stir until well coated with the sauce.
4. Cover and cook for 3 1/2 hour on HIGH.
5. After 3 1/2 hours, add the cornstarch. Stir well.

6. Cover and cook for another 30 minutes.
7. Season with salt to taste and then serve warm with rice.

Parsnip, Turnip, Carrot, Apricot, and Prune Tagine

Prep Time: 50 minutes; **Cook Time:** 9 hours

Serving Size: 300 g; **Serves:** 8; **Calories:** 177

Total Fat: 0.9 g **Saturated Fat:** 0 g; **Trans Fat:** 0 g

Protein: 3.9 g; **Total Carbs:** 41.8 g

Dietary Fiber: 8.2 g; **Sugars:** 21.2 g

Cholesterol: 0 mg; **Sodium:** 243 mg; **Potassium:** 854 mg;

Vitamin A: 205%; **Vitamin C:** 52%; **Calcium:** 9%; **Iron:** 8%

Ingredients:

- ☐ 1 pound parsnips, peeled and diced
- ☐ 1 pound turnips, peeled and diced
- ☐ 1 pound carrots, peeled and diced
- ☐ 6 dried apricots, chopped
- ☐ 4 prunes, pitted, chopped
- ☐ 2 onions, medium-sized, chopped
- ☐ 1 teaspoon ground turmeric
- ☐ 1 teaspoon ground cumin
- ☐ 1/2 teaspoon ground ginger
- ☐ 1/2 teaspoon ground cinnamon
- ☐ 1/4 teaspoon ground cayenne pepper
- ☐ 1 tablespoon dried parsley
- ☐ 1 tablespoon dried cilantro
- ☐ 1 can (14 ounce) vegetable broth

Directions:

1. Put the prunes, apricots, carrots, onions, turnips, and parsnips into the slow cooker. Toss to combine.
2. Season with cilantro, parsley, cayenne pepper, cinnamon, ginger, cumin, and turmeric and then pour the broth into the cooker.
3. Cover and cook for 9 hours on LOW.

Potato, Navy Beans, and Carrots Cassoulet

Prep Time: 20 minutes; **Cook Time:** 9 hours on LOW	

Serving Size: 124 g; **Serves:** 8; **Calories:** 289

Total Fat: 5 g **Saturated Fat**: 0.9 g; **Trans Fat**: 0 g

Protein: 14.6 g; **Total Carbs:** 48.8 g

Dietary Fiber: 16.1 g; **Sugars:** 4.1 g

Cholesterol: 0 mg; **Sodium:** 792 mg; **Potassium**: 876 mg;

Vitamin A: 53%; **Vitamin C**: 17%; **Calcium**: 14%; **Iron**: 24%

Ingredients:

- ☐ 1 potato, large-sized, peeled and cubed
- ☐ 1 pound dry navy beans, soaked overnight
- ☐ 2 carrots, peeled and diced
- ☐ 1 sprig fresh lemon thyme, chopped
- ☐ 1 sprig fresh rosemary
- ☐ 1 sprig fresh savory
- ☐ 2 tablespoons olive oil
- ☐ 4 cups mushroom broth
- ☐ 4 sprigs fresh parsley
- ☐ 1 onion
- ☐ 1 cube vegetable bouillon
- ☐ 1 bay leaf

Directions:

1. In a skillet, heat a bit of oil over medium heat. Add the onion and carrots; cook, stirring, until tender. Transfer into the slow cooker.
2. Add the carrots, bouillon, broth, and bay leaf. If needed, add water to cover all the ingredients in the cooker. Tie together the savory, thyme, rosemary, and parsley. Add into the pot.
3. Cover and cook for 8 hours on LOW.
4. Stir in the potato. Cook for 1 more hour.
5. Just before serving, remove the herbs.

Mushroom Stroganoff

Prep Time: 5 minutes; **Cook Time:** 4 hours on HIGH

Serving Size: 489 g; **Serves:** 2; **Calories:** 122

Total Fat: 2.6 g **Saturated Fat:** 0.8 g; **Trans Fat:** 0 g

Protein: 11.5 g; **Total Carbs:** 19.5 g

Dietary Fiber: 5.9 g; **Sugars:** 8.6 g

Cholesterol: 3 mg; **Sodium:** 85 mg; **Potassium:** 1153 mg;

Vitamin A: 36%; **Vitamin C:** 42%; **Calcium:** 4%; **Iron:** 54%

Ingredients:

- ☐ 600 grams mushrooms, diced (leave the very small ones whole; half- or quarter-dice the larger ones)
- ☐ 3 cloves garlic, minced
- ☐ 250 ml (1 cup) vegetable stock
- ☐ 2 teaspoons smoked paprika
- ☐ 1 onion, halved and thinly sliced
- ☐ 4 tablespoons fresh parsley, chopped
- ☐ 1 heaped tablespoon cashew sour cream
- ☐ Salt and black pepper, to taste

Directions:

1. Put the mushrooms, garlic, stock, paprika, and onion into the slow cooker. Stir well to mix.
2. Cover and cook for 4 hours on HIGH.
3. After cooking time, stir in the sour cream and then season to taste. Serve with your choice of carbohydrate. Garnish each serving with fresh parsley.

Cauliflower Bolognese Zucchini Noodles

Prep Time: 10 minutes; **Cook Time:** 3 hours, 30 minutes	

Prep Time: 10 minutes; **Cook Time:** 3 hours, 30 minutes

Serving Size: 456 g; **Serves:** 5-6; **Calories:** 90

Total Fat: 1 g **Saturated Fat:** 0 g; **Trans Fat:** 0 g

Protein: 5.7 g; **Total Carbs:** 18.5 g

Dietary Fiber: 6.2 g; **Sugars:** 10 g

Cholesterol: 0 mg; **Sodium:** 121 mg; **Potassium:** 1123 mg;

Vitamin A: 39%; **Vitamin C:** 155%; **Calcium:** 7%; **Iron:** 10%

Ingredients:

For the Bolognese:
- ☐ 1 head cauliflower, cut up into florets
- ☐ 1 teaspoon dried basil flakes
- ☐ 1/2 cup vegetable broth, low-sodium
- ☐ 1/4 teaspoon red pepper flakes
- ☐ 2 cans (14 ounces) diced tomatoes, no salt added
- ☐ 2 garlic cloves, small-sized, minced
- ☐ 2 teaspoons dried oregano flakes
- ☐ 3/4 cup red onion, diced
- ☐ Salt and pepper, to taste

For the pasta:
- ☐ 5 zucchinis, large-sized, noodled

Directions:

1. Put the Bolognese ingredients into the slow cooker.
2. Cover and cook for 3 1/2 hours on HIGH.
3. After cooking time, mash the cauliflower using a fork or a potato masher until the florets break into a Bolognese texture.

Thai Spaghetti Squash Noodle Bowl

Prep Time: 20 minutes; **Cook Time:** 8 to 9 hours on LOW

Serving Size: 1322 g; **Serves:** 2; **Calories:** 684

Total Fat: 38.5 g **Saturated Fat:** 7.4 g; **Trans Fat:** 0 g

Protein: 13.9 g; **Total Carbs:** 81.5 g

Dietary Fiber: 4 g; **Sugars:** 9.8 g

Cholesterol: 0 mg; **Sodium:** 1300 mg; **Potassium:** 1441 mg;

Vitamin A: 20%; **Vitamin C:** 169%; **Calcium:** 32%; **Iron:** 33%

Ingredients:
- ☐ 1 spaghetti squash, small-sized (about 4-5 pounds)
- ☐ 2 cups broccoli, steamed
- ☐ 1/2 Thai peanut dressing (I used lime juice instead 1/2 of vinegar)
- ☐ 1 tablespoon sesame seeds
- ☐ 2 cups water

For the Thai peanut dressing:
- ☐ 3 tablespoons vegetable oil
- ☐ 3 tablespoons rice wine vinegar
- ☐ 2 tablespoons peanut butter
- ☐ 2 cloves garlic, minced
- ☐ 1/2 teaspoon salt
- ☐ 1 teaspoon sesame oil
- ☐ 1 tablespoon soy sauce, reduced sodium
- ☐ 1 tablespoon ginger root, grated
- ☐ 1 1/2 tablespoon light brown sugar, packed
- ☐ 1/2 teaspoon sriracha, optional
- ☐ 1/2 teaspoon sesame seeds, for serving, optional

Toppings (optional):
- ☐ Peanuts, chopped
- ☐ Sriracha

Directions:
1. Using a fork, pierce the spaghetti squash all over, the way you would with a potato before baking.
2. Put the spaghetti squash into the slow cooker. Pour 2 cups of water.

3. Cover and cook for 8 to 9 hours on LOW. The outside of the squash will turn brownish and dingy while cooking, so don't worry. The insides will be perfectly fine.
4. After cooking time, remove the squash from the slow cooker. Let cool for about 20 to 30 minutes. Discard the water.
5. Meanwhile, prepare the broccoli or the dressing. To prepare the dressing, whisk all the sauce ingredients in a small-sized bowl until well combined. If possible, refrigerate for a couple of hours before using.
6. When the squash is cooled, cut into halves. Scoop out the seeds and the pulp and discard.
7. With a fork, shred the spaghetti into noodle-like strands. Shred all the way to the flesh, if desired.
8. Put the spaghetti squash strands into bowls. Top each serving with 1 cup of broccoli, 3 tablespoons of sauce, and garnish with 1/2 tablespoon of sesame seeds and peanuts, if desired.

White Bean Cassoulet with Carrots and Diced Tomatoes

Prep Time: 30 minutes; **Cook Time:** 4-6 hours on LOW	

Serving Size: 394 g; **Serves**: 6; **Calories:** 650
Total Fat: 7.9 g **Saturated Fat**: 1.4 g; **Trans Fat**: 0 g
Protein: 37.6 g; **Total Carbs:** 112 g
Dietary Fiber: 25.3 g; **Sugars:** 9.7 g
Cholesterol: 2 mg; **Sodium**: 226 mg; **Potassium**: 2939 mg;
Vitamin A: 99%; **Vitamin C**: 38%; **Calcium**: 43%; **Iron**: 95%

Ingredients:

For the cassoulet:

- [ ] 2 cans (15 ounces each) white beans, your choice, rinsed and drained
- [ ] 1 can (15 ounces) diced tomatoes
- [ ] 2 carrots, large-sized, sliced
- [ ] 4 cloves garlic, minced
- [ ] 3 leeks, white parts, sliced
- [ ] 2 stalks celery, diced
- [ ] 2 cups vegetable stock
- [ ] 1 tablespoons Italian seasoning
- [ ] 1 bay leaf

For the breadcrumbs:

- [ ] 1 clove garlic, minced (or garlic powder)
- [ ] 1 cup coarse bread crumbs, good quality
- [ ] 1 lemon, zested
- [ ] 1/4 cup fresh parsley, finely chopped
- [ ] 2 tablespoons olive oil

Directions:

For the cassoulet:
1. Add a little water or broth into a large-sized skillet and heat over medium heat. Add the celery and the leeks. Cook until soft. Add the carrots. Cook until slightly browned, adding more broth or water in the skillet, if necessary.
2. Add the garlic. Cook for 1 minute more. Season with salt and pepper to taste.

3. Transfer the veggie mixture into the slow cooker. Add the rest of the cassoulet ingredients.
4. Cover and cook for 4 to 6 hours on LOW or until the vegetables are tender. To thicken the cassoulet, slightly mash some of the beans.

For the breadcrumbs:
1. Toss the breadcrumbs with the garlic or garlic powder and then layer evenly in a baking sheet. Slightly toast in a 350F for about 10 minutes. Let cool. When cool, combine with the lemon zest and the parsley.

To serve:
Spoon the cassoulet into individual ramekins. Sprinkle the top with the toasted breadcrumbs. Alternatively, sprinkle toasted breadcrumbs directly in the slow cooker with the cassoulet. Serve.

Tofu, Eggplant, Peas, and Bell Peppers Vegetable Curry

Prep Time: 30 minutes; **Cook Time:** 3-4 hours		

Prep Time: 30 minutes; **Cook Time:** 3-4 hours

Serving Size: 502 g; **Serves:** 4; **Calories:** 252

Total Fat: 10.8 g **Saturated Fat:** 6 g; **Trans Fat**: 0 g

Protein: 15.3 g; **Total Carbs:** 29 g

Dietary Fiber: 7.9 g; **Sugars:** 12.5 g

Cholesterol: 0 mg; **Sodium:** 1209 mg; **Potassium:** 700 mg;

Vitamin A: 79%; **Vitamin C:** 172%; **Calcium:** 28%; **Iron:** 22%

Ingredients:
- ☐ 16 ounces tofu, extra-firm, drained and pressed
- ☐ 1 eggplant, small-sized, chopped
- ☐ 3/4 cup peas
- ☐ 1 can (14.5 ounces) lite coconut milk (or full fat)
- ☐ 1 1/2 cups bell pepper, sliced (I used frozen)
- ☐ 1/4 cup Thai curry paste (green or red)
- ☐ 1/2 teaspoon turmeric
- ☐ 1 teaspoon salt
- ☐ 1 tablespoon fresh minced ginger
- ☐ 1 tablespoon coconut sugar
- ☐ 1 onion, medium-sized, chopped
- ☐ 1 cup vegetable broth
- ☐ Quinoa or brown rice, for serving, optional

Directions:
1. Remove the tofu from the package and drain. Put in a tofu press and set the press in a baking sheet or a plate to catch the liquid. Tighten the knobs until the tofu is snug. Press for 30 to 60 minutes, tightening the knobs as needed. Alternatively, put the tofu between clean kitchen towels or paper towels. Place on a plate.
2. Top the towel-covered tofu with a couple of books or any heavy object. Let press for 30-60 minutes.
3. Meanwhile, put the coconut sugar, salt, turmeric, ginger, curry paste, vegetable broth, and coconut milk in the slow cooker. Whisk well until combined.
4. Add the eggplant, peas, bell pepper, and onion. Stir to combine.

5. Cover and cook for 3 to 4 hours on HIGH.
6. While the vegetable mix is cooking, spray a large-sized pan with olive oil and heat over medium heat.
7. Cut the tofu into bite-sized pieces. Working in batches, cook the tofu pieces in the pan for a couple of minutes per side until all the sides are golden. Set aside until ready to use.
8. During the last 30 minutes of cooking the curry, add the friend tofu into the slow cooker and let cook for 30 minutes.
9. Serve over quinoa or brown rice, if desired.

Vegan Jambalaya

Prep Time: 20 minutes; **Cook Time:** 4-6 hours on LOW; 2 hours on HIGH

Serving Size: 178 g; **Serves:** 10 cups; **Calories:** 229

Total Fat: 0.7 g **Saturated Fat:** 0 g; **Trans Fat:** 0 g

Protein: 5.6 g; **Total Carbs:** 49.1 g

Dietary Fiber: 1.6 g; **Sugars:** 1.4 g

Cholesterol: 0 mg; **Sodium:** 371 mg; **Potassium:** 250 mg;

Vitamin A: 16%; **Vitamin C:** 49%; **Calcium:** 4%; **Iron:** 16%

Ingredients:

- ☐ 1 can (16-ounces) diced tomatoes with green chilies
- ☐ 1 cup okra, diced
- ☐ 1 1/2 cups vegetable broth
- ☐ 1 green bell pepper, diced
- ☐ 1/2 onion, diced
- ☐ 1/2 teaspoon paprika
- ☐ 1/4 teaspoon cayenne pepper
- ☐ 1/4 teaspoon ground black pepper
- ☐ 1/4 teaspoon salt
- ☐ 2 cloves garlic, minced
- ☐ 3 celery ribs (around 1 1/2 cups), diced
- ☐ 3 cups cilantro rice, cooked
- ☐ 6 ounces soy chorizo, optional

Directions:

1. Cook the chorizo in a skillet over medium-high heat until brown. Transfer into the slow cooker.
2. Add garlic, celery, onion, okra, and bell pepper into the slow cooker. Pour in the broth and the diced tomatoes. Add the seasoning and stir to combine.
3. Cover and cook for 4-6 hours on LOW or for 2 hours on HIGH.

Teriyaki Tofu

Prep Time: 30 minutes; **Cook Time:** 8-10 hours on LOW

Serving Size: 439 g; **Serves:** 4; **Calories:** 329

Total Fat: 13.3 g **Saturated Fat:** 2.5 g; **Trans Fat:** 0 g

Protein: 23.7 g; **Total Carbs:** 32.5 g

Dietary Fiber: 3.3 g; **Sugars:** 20.8 g

Cholesterol: 0 mg; **Sodium:** 2267 mg; **Potassium:** 597 mg;

Vitamin A: 1%; **Vitamin C:** 45%; **Calcium:** 49%; **Iron:** 28%

Ingredients:
- [ ] 2 packages (1 pound each) tofu, firm or extra firm
- [ ] 6 pineapple rings, canned or fresh
- [ ] 1 cup pineapple juice
- [ ] 1 tablespoon ginger, grated, less or more to taste
- [ ] 1 tablespoon sesame oil
- [ ] 1/2 cup tamari or coconut aminos
- [ ] 1/2 cup vegetable broth
- [ ] 1/4 cup mirin
- [ ] 1/4 cup unseasoned rice vinegar
- [ ] 2 tablespoon brown sugar
- [ ] 3-4 cloves garlic, minced very finely or grated
- [ ] Fresh kale, shredded, for serving
- [ ] Rice, for serving

Directions:
1. Drain the tofu. Cut each block into 6 rectangular pieces. Press the tofu pieces to squeeze out excess water. Cut the pressed tofu into halves to make squares and then cut them diagonally to make triangles. Set aside until needed.
2. In a medium bowl, whisk the juice with the broth, mirin, tamari, sugar, vinegar, ginger, oil, and garlic.
3. Put the pineapple into the slow cooker. Place the tofu triangles on top of the pineapple. Pour the prepared sauce over the tofu.
4. Cover and cook for 8-10 hours on LOW.

Notes: You can prepare the tofu ahead of time. Keep them in the refrigerator for up to 2 days until cooking.

Pot Pie

Prep Time: 20 minutes; **Cook Time:** 6-8 hours on LOW, plus 30 minutes on HIGH

Serving Size: 588 g; **Serves:** 4; **Calories:** 452

Total Fat: 24.7 g **Saturated Fat:** 9.8 g; **Trans Fat:** 0 g

Protein: 19.5 g; **Total Carbs:** 45.2 g

Dietary Fiber: 8.3 g; **Sugars:** 8.4 g

Cholesterol: 0 mg; **Sodium:** 639 mg; **Potassium:** 1105 mg;

Vitamin A: 104%; **Vitamin C:** 40%; **Calcium:** 36%; **Iron:** 43%

Ingredients:

For the stew:

- [ ] 1 1/2 cups cubed seitan (chicken-flavored) OR vegan sausage, crumbled, OR tofu, diced OR bean OR potatoes, diced (I used 1 package (15 ounces) firm tofu, cubed and baked)
- [ ] 1 cup water, or more as needed
- [ ] 1 onion, small-sized, minced
- [ ] 1 pound frozen mixed vegetables (carrots, green beans, corn, and peas)
- [ ] 1 stalk celery, large-sized, minced, optional
- [ ] 1 teaspoon dried thyme
- [ ] 10 ounces packaged sliced mushrooms
- [ ] 2 cloves garlic, minced
- [ ] 2 tablespoons flour, to thicken, if needed (or coconut flour)
- [ ] 2 tablespoons vegan bouillon, chicken-flavored (or 1 1/2 cups vegetable broth plus 1 cup water instead of bouillon and water, for a total of 2 1/2 cups liquid)
- [ ] Salt and pepper, to taste

For the biscuits:

- [ ] 1 cup whole-wheat, white, or gluten-free flour (I used 1/2 cup whole-wheat pastry flour plus 1/2 cup cornmeal)
- [ ] 1/2 cup non-dairy milk, plain, unsweetened (I used almond milk)
- [ ] 1 1/2 teaspoons baking powder
- [ ] 1/2 teaspoon dried thyme, optional

- ☐ 1/2 teaspoon salt
- ☐ 3 tablespoons olive oil (I used just 2 tablespoons)

Directions:

The night before:
1. Put the seitan, celery, garlic, and onion in a large-sized, airtight container and keep in the refrigerator.

In the morning:
2. Lightly grease the slow cooker with nonstick cooking spray.
3. Except for the flour, combine all the stew ingredients in the slow cooker. If cooking for more than 8 hours, then add more water in the slow cooker. Stir to combine.
4. Cover and cook for 6-8 hours on LOW.
5. About half an hour before serving, add water if the mixture seems too thick. If desired, thicken the mixture with the flour. Taste and, if needed, adjust seasonings.

To make the biscuits:
1. Combine all of the ingredients in a bowl, adding a little milk at a time. Knead until the mixture is formed into dough. Turn the dough onto a floured cutting board. Roll into 1/2-inch thickness. With the rim of a glass, cut the thinned dough into circles. Put the dough circles into the slow cooker, placing them on top of the filling.
2. Set the slow cooker to HIGH. Place a clean dishtowel over the slow cooker and close the lid. Cook for 30 minutes more.

Notes: To bake the tofu, preheat the oven to 475F. Drain the tofu and then cut into cubes. Grease a large-sized baking dish with nonstick cooking spray. In a single layer, put the tofu in the greased dish. Lightly spray the tofu with cooking spray. Bake for about 25 to 30 minutes, turning 2 to 3 times, until the tofu cubes are browned and crisped.

Puttanesca Pizza

Prep Time: 30 minutes, plus dough rising; **Cook Time:** 1 hour; 45 minutes on HIGH

Serving Size: 279 g; **Serves:** 2-4; **Calories:** 485	
Total Fat: 12.1 g **Saturated Fat:** 1.7 g; **Trans Fat:** 0 g	
Protein: 13 g; **Total Carbs:** 81.7 g	
Dietary Fiber: 6.7 g; **Sugars:** 4.5 g	
Cholesterol: 1 mg; **Sodium:** 1211 mg; **Potassium:** 190 mg;	
Vitamin A: 21%; **Vitamin C:** 14%; **Calcium:** 10%; **Iron:** 42%	

Ingredients:
For the dough:
- [ ] 1 1/2 cups unbleached all-purpose flour
- [ ] 1 1/2 teaspoon instant yeast
- [ ] 1 tablespoon olive oil
- [ ] 1/2 cup warm water, or as needed
- [ ] 1/2 teaspoon Italian seasoning
- [ ] 1/2 teaspoon salt

For the sauce:
- [ ] 1 tablespoon capers, rinsed and drained
- [ ] 1 tablespoon fresh flat-leaf parsley, chopped
- [ ] 1/2 cup crushed tomatoes
- [ ] 1/4 cup green olives, pitted, sliced
- [ ] 1/4 cup Kalamata olives, pitted, sliced
- [ ] 1/4 teaspoon dried basil
- [ ] 1/4 teaspoon dried oregano
- [ ] 1/4 teaspoon garlic powder
- [ ] 1/4 teaspoon hot red pepper flakes
- [ ] 1/4 teaspoon sugar
- [ ] Salt and fresh ground black pepper
- [ ] 1/2 cup vegan mozzarella cheese, shredded, optional

Directions:
1. Lightly grease a large-sized bowl with oil. In a food processor, combine the flour with the yeast, Italian seasoning, and salt. With the motor running, add the olive oil through the feed tube. Slowly add as much water to form a sticky dough ball. Transfer the dough onto a

floured surface. Knead the dough for about 1-2 minutes or until elastic and smooth. Shape the dough into a bowl and put into the greased bowl, turning it to coat the entire surface with oil. Cover the bowl with plastic wrap and set aside for 1 hour at warm room temperature until it doubles in size.

2. Meanwhile, prepare the sauce. Combine the tomatoes with the olives, parsley, capers, oregano, basil, sugar, garlic powder, salt, red pepper flakes, and black pepper to taste.

3. Generously grease a 5- to 7-quart slow cooker with nonstick cooking spray.

4. Punch down the dough and then transfer onto a floured surface. Flatten the dough and then shape it to fit the slow cooker. Put the dough in the slow cooker. Spread the prepared sauce over the dough.

5. To prevent the condensation from dripping onto the pizza, drape a clean kitchen towel over the cooker and then cover with the lid.

6. Cook for 1 hour and 45 minutes on HIGH.

7. If adding vegan mozzarella pizza, sprinkle it over the pizza after 1 hour and 15 minutes of cooking. Continue cooking for 30 minutes more until the cheese is melted.

Mushroom, Kidney Bean, Zucchini, and Okra Vegetarian Gumbo

Prep Time: 20 minutes; **Cook Time:** 6-8 hours on LOW	

Prep Time: 20 minutes; **Cook Time:** 6-8 hours on LOW

Serving Size: 544 g; **Serves:** 4-6; **Calories:** 533

Total Fat: 9.5 g **Saturated Fat:** 1.4 g; **Trans Fat:** 0 g

Protein: 31.4 g; **Total Carbs:** 85.4 g

Dietary Fiber: 20.6 g; **Sugars:** 11.8 g

Cholesterol: 0 mg; **Sodium:** 538 mg; **Potassium:** 2308 mg;

Vitamin A: 43%; **Vitamin C:** 159%; **Calcium:** 15%; **Iron:** 57%

Ingredients:
- ☐ 8 ounces white mushrooms, quartered
- ☐ 1 can (14.5-ounce) diced tomatoes
- ☐ 1 can (15-ounce) kidney beans, rinsed and drained
- ☐ 1 cup sliced frozen okra
- ☐ 1 zucchini, small-sized, cut into thick half moons
- ☐ 1 green bell pepper, chopped
- ☐ 1 tablespoon Cajun seasoning
- ☐ 1 yellow onion, chopped
- ☐ 2 cups vegetable broth
- ☐ 2 stalks celery, chopped
- ☐ 2 tablespoons all-purpose flour
- ☐ 2 tablespoons olive oil
- ☐ 2 tablespoons vegan Worcestershire sauce
- ☐ 3 cloves garlic, minced
- ☐ 1 bay leaf
- ☐ Cooked rice and hot sauce, for serving
- ☐ Salt and pepper, to taste

Directions:
1. Pour 1 tablespoon oil into a Dutch oven and heat over medium heat. Add the garlic, celery, bell pepper, and onion. Cook for about 8 to 10 minutes or until the vegetables are starting to brown ad soften. Transfer the mix into a 4- to 6-quart slow cooker.
2. Return the Dutch oven on the stovetop. Add the remaining oil and heat. Stir the flour in the Dutch oven. Stirring constantly, cook for about 5 minutes or until the flour is golden brown. Add the broth and bring the mix to

a boil. When boiling, carefully transfer the mix into the slow cooker.
3. Except for the cooked rice and the hot sauce, add the remaining ingredients into the slow cooker.
4. Cover and cook for 6-8 hours on LOW. When the cooking time is up, remove the bay leaf. Taste and, if needed, season with salt and pepper.
5. Serve over hot cooked rice with the hot sauce.

Indian-Inspired Chickpeas and Red Potatoes

Prep Time: 20 minutes; **Cook Time:** 4 hours	
Serving Size: 552 g; **Serves**: 4; **Calories:** 933	
Total Fat: 16.3 g **Saturated Fat**: 1.9 g; **Trans Fat**: 0 g	
Protein: 46.4 g; **Total Carbs:** 158.5 g	
Dietary Fiber: 41.8 g; **Sugars:** 29.3 g	
Cholesterol: 0 mg; **Sodium:** 847 mg; **Potassium:** 2853 mg;	
Vitamin A: 25%; **Vitamin C**: 70%; **Calcium**: 28%; **Iron**: 88%	

Ingredients:

- ☐ 1 can (15-ounce) diced tomatoes
- ☐ 1 pound red potatoes, cut into 1/2-inch cubes
- ☐ 2 cans (15-ounce each) chickpeas, drained and rinsed
- ☐ 1 cup vegetable broth
- ☐ 1 lime
- ☐ 1 teaspoon kosher salt
- ☐ 1 yellow onion, medium-sized, diced (about 2 cups)
- ☐ 1/2 teaspoon garam masala
- ☐ 1/2 teaspoon ground ginger
- ☐ 1/4 teaspoon crushed red pepper flakes
- ☐ 1/4 teaspoon turmeric
- ☐ 2 cloves garlic, medium-sized, minced (about 2 teaspoons)
- ☐ 2 tablespoons tomato paste
- ☐ 2 teaspoons ground coriander
- ☐ 2 teaspoons ground cumin
- ☐ 2 teaspoons olive oil
- ☐ Small bunch fresh cilantro

Directions:

1. Into a large-sized sauté pan, drizzle the olive oil and heat over medium heat, swirling the pan to coat with the oil. Add the onion and occasionally stirring, cook for about 5 minutes or until translucent.
2. Add the coriander, garlic, garam masala, cumin, turmeric, ginger, salt, and pepper flakes. Stirring occasionally, cook for 1 minute. Add the tomato paste, diced tomatoes, and broth. Stir well until combined. Pour the mixture into a 3-

quart or larger-sized slow cooker. Stir in the potatoes and the chickpeas.

3. Cover and cook for 4-5 hours on HIGH or for 8-10 hours on LOW, or until the potatoes are fork tender.

4. Ladle the dish into serving bowls. Serve with fresh lime wedges and cilantro.

Mushroom Stroganoff

Prep Time: 15 minutes; **Cook Time:** 4 hours on HIGH	
Serving Size: 451 g; **Serves:** 3; **Calories:** 146	
Total Fat: 8.2 g **Saturated Fat**: 4.6 g; **Trans Fat**: 0 g	
Protein: 7.4 g; **Total Carbs:** 15.2 g	
Dietary Fiber: 3.7 g; **Sugars:** 7.3 g	
Cholesterol: 17 mg; **Sodium**: 397 mg; **Potassium**: 771 mg;	
Vitamin A: 45%; **Vitamin C**: 41%; **Calcium**: 6%; **Iron**: 34%	

Ingredients:
- ☐ 500 grams mushrooms, sliced
- ☐ 4 tablespoons sour cream, heaping-full
- ☐ 3 teaspoons paprika
- ☐ 3 cloves garlic, thinly sliced
- ☐ 2 tablespoons tomato ketchup
- ☐ 1 tablespoon butter
- ☐ 1 stock cube, dissolved in 600 ml hot water
- ☐ 1 onion, diced
- ☐ Handful fresh parsley, chopped

Directions:
1. Melt the butter in a large-sized pan. Add the mushroom and the onion, cook for about 5 to 10 minutes or until they start to shrink and are slightly soft, but are still not thoroughly cooked. Transfer the mixture into the slow cooker.
2. Add the stock, garlic, paprika, and ketchup into the slow cooker and stir to combine.
3. Cover and cook for 4 hours on HIGH.
4. When the cooking time is up, stir in the vegan sour cream and parsley.

Notes: This stroganoff is good as is. If you want your dish thicker, transfer into a saucepan and simmer for about 10 minutes.

Side Dishes

Maple Bourbon Baked Beans

Prep Time: 15 minutes; **Cook Time:** 12-16 hours	
Serving Size: 244 g; **Serves:** 8; **Calories:** 593	
Total Fat: 8.6 g **Saturated Fat:** 1.2 g; **Trans Fat:** 0 g	
Protein: 14.2 g; **Total Carbs:** 102.5 g	
Dietary Fiber: 12.4 g; **Sugars:** 58.3 g	
Cholesterol: 0 mg; **Sodium:** 707 mg; **Potassium:** 1184 mg;	
Vitamin A: 3%; **Vitamin C:** 8%; **Calcium:** 19%; **Iron:** 27%	

Ingredients:
- ☐ 1 pound dry Great Northern beans (or navy beans)
- ☐ 1 cup barbeque sauce
- ☐ 1 cup bourbon
- ☐ 1 cup light brown sugar, packed
- ☐ 1 cup maple syrup
- ☐ 1 cup water
- ☐ 1/4 cup apple cider vinegar
- ☐ 1/4 cup ketchup, heaping
- ☐ 1/4 cup molasses (use light/mild/medium, not robust/dark/ blackstrap)
- ☐ 1/4 cup mustard (I used yellow; use less if using Dijon or stoneground)
- ☐ 1/4 cup olive oil
- ☐ 2 tablespoons liquid aminos or tamari

Directions:
1. Put the dry beans in a colander. Rinse and sort over the sink. Put the beans in a large-sized pot. Cover with 8 cups of water and let soak for at least 8 hours or overnight. Alternatively, you can use the rapid soak method. Bring the beans, with 8 cups of water, to a boil and boil rapidly, uncovered, for 3 minutes. Turn off the heat, cover the pot, and let stand for 1 hour.
2. After soaking, drain and rinse well in a colander under running water over the sink.

3. Return the rinsed soaked beans into the pot. Cover with 6 cups of water and simmer over low heat for about 45 minutes or until 80% cooked.
4. Meanwhile, combine the remaining ingredients in the slow cooker. Whisk until smooth.
5. When the beans are simmered, drain, and then add into the slow cooker. Stir to coat.
6. Cover and cook for about 12 hours on LOW or until the beans are tender and the sauce is reduced and thick. Check after 8 hours into cooking.
7. If the sauce is not reduced and thick after 12 hours, remove the lid. Increase the heat to HIGH and cook for 4 more hours.
8. Serve immediately.

Notes: Store the beans in airtight containers and keep in the fridge for up to 1 week. These beans taste even better after 2-3 days when the flavors develop even more.

No Refrying Refried Beans

Prep Time: 15 minutes; **Cook Time:** 8 hours on HIGH	

Prep Time: 15 minutes; **Cook Time:** 8 hours on HIGH

Serving Size: 192 g; **Serves:** 15; **Calories:** 139

Total Fat: 0.5 g **Saturated Fat:** 0 g; **Trans Fat:** 0 g

Protein: 8.5 g; **Total Carbs:** 25.4 g

Dietary Fiber: 6.2 g; **Sugars:** 1.2 g

Cholesterol: 0 mg; **Sodium:** 785 mg; **Potassium:** 559 mg;

Vitamin A: 0%; **Vitamin C:** 6%; **Calcium:** 5%; **Iron:** 12%

Ingredients:
- ☐ 3 cups dry pinto beans, rinsed
- ☐ 2 tablespoons garlic, minced
- ☐ 1/8 teaspoon ground cumin, optional
- ☐ 1/2 fresh jalapeno pepper, seeded and chopped
- ☐ 1 onion, peeled and halved
- ☐ 1 3/4 teaspoons black pepper, fresh ground
- ☐ 5 teaspoons salt
- ☐ 9 cups water

Directions:
1. Put the beans, cumin, pepper, salt, garlic, jalapeno, and onion into the slow cooker.
2. Pour thee water in the cooker and stir to mix.
3. Cover and cook for 8 hours on HIGH. If needed, add more water during cooking.
4. When the beans are cooked, strain and reserve the cooking liquid. With a potato masher, mash the beans. Add reserved cooking liquid as needed to reach your desired consistency.

Easy Saag Aloo

Prep Time: 5 minutes; **Cook Time:** 3 hours on HIGH

Serving Size: 341 g; **Serves:** 3-4; **Calories:** 220

Total Fat: 5.3 g **Saturated Fat:** 0.7 g; **Trans Fat:** 0 g

Protein: 6.4 g; **Total Carbs:** 39.3 g

Dietary Fiber: 7.6 g; **Sugars:** 3.8 g

Cholesterol: 0 mg; **Sodium:** 199 mg; **Potassium:** 1392 mg;

Vitamin A: 159%; **Vitamin C:** 113%; **Calcium:** 11%; **Iron:** 21%

Ingredients:

- [ ] 650 grams potatoes, peeled and cut into 1-inch chunks
- [ ] 250 grams fresh spinach, roughly chopped
- [ ] 50 ml water
- [ ] 1/2 vegetable stock cube, crumbled
- [ ] 1/2 teaspoon hot chili powder
- [ ] 1/2 teaspoon garam masala
- [ ] 1/2 teaspoon cumin
- [ ] 1/2 onion, thinly sliced
- [ ] 1/1 teaspoon ground coriander
- [ ] 1 tablespoon oil
- [ ] Black pepper

Directions:

1. Put the potatoes into the slow cooker. Add the rest of the ingredients, leaving the spinach for last, topping it on top of the ingredients. Add as much spinach as you can fit into your slow cooker – just add the rest of the spinach about 1 hour into cooking time.
2. Cover and cook for 3 hours on HIGH or until the potatoes are cooked. Stir and scrape down the sides every hour or so.

Baked Beans Coconut Curry

Prep Time: 10 minutes; **Cook Time:** 8-10 hours on LOW	

Serving Size: 250 g; **Serves:** 6-8; **Calories:** 669

Total Fat: 20.1 g **Saturated Fat:** 14.7 g; **Trans Fat:** 0 g

Protein: 30.8 g; **Total Carbs:** 95.6 g

Dietary Fiber: 23.4 g; **Sugars:** 12.1 g

Cholesterol: 0 mg; **Sodium:** 250 mg; **Potassium:** 2318 mg;

Vitamin A: 9%; **Vitamin C:** 30%; **Calcium:** 18%; **Iron:** 50%

Ingredients:
- ☐ 4 cups pinto beans, cooked (or 3cans (15-ounce each), drained and rinsed)
- ☐ 1 can (14-ounce) light coconut milk
- ☐ 1 can (6-ounce) tomato paste
- ☐ 1 clove garlic, medium-sized, minced (about 1 teaspoon)
- ☐ 1 tablespoon fresh ginger, minced (about half of a thumb-sized piece)
- ☐ 1 tablespoon olive oil
- ☐ 1 yellow onion, medium-sized, diced
- ☐ 1/2 teaspoon cumin
- ☐ 1/2 teaspoon salt (I used kosher salt)
- ☐ 1/8 teaspoon red pepper flakes, crushed
- ☐ 2 tablespoons brown sugar (dark or light)
- ☐ 3 teaspoons curry powder

Directions:
1. Put the beans in a 3-quart or larger-sized slow cooker.
2. Into a large-sized skillet, add the oil and heat over medium heat.
3. Add the onion and sauté for 5 minutes or until starting to soften.
4. Add the garlic and sauté for 1 minute. Stir in the minced ginger, red peppers, cumin, and salt.
5. Reduce the heat to low. Stir in the tomato paste, coconut milk, and brown sugar until evenly combined. Pour the mixture over the beans in the cooker. Toss until the beans are evenly coated.
6. Cover and cook for 8-10 hours on LOW.

7. After cooking time, taste and, if needed, season with more salt.

Mango and Bourbon Baked Beans

Prep Time: 45 minutes; plus overnight soaking **Cook Time:** 6-8 hours on LOW

Serving Size: 116 g; **Serves:** 16; **Calories:** 247	

Serving Size: 116 g; **Serves:** 16; **Calories:** 247

Total Fat: 1.1 g **Saturated Fat:** 0 g; **Trans Fat:** 0 g

Protein: 12.9 g; **Total Carbs:** 47.1 g

Dietary Fiber: 14.4 g; **Sugars:** 11.8 g

Cholesterol: 0 mg; **Sodium:** 266 mg; **Potassium:** 768 mg;

Vitamin A: 3%; **Vitamin C:** 10%; **Calcium:** 9%; **Iron:** 18%

Ingredients:
- ☐ 2 bags (16 ounces each) dried navy beans
- ☐ 1 mango, peeled, diced, and pureed
- ☐ 1 1/2 cup barbecue sauce
- ☐ 1 1/2 tablespoons bourbon
- ☐ 1 1/4 cup water
- ☐ 1 onion, large-sized, chopped
- ☐ 1 teaspoon maple syrup
- ☐ 1/4 teaspoon chipotle powder (or 1/2 teaspoon more for a spicier dish)
- ☐ 2 tablespoons balsamic vinegar
- ☐ Cooking spray
- ☐ Salt and pepper, to taste

Directions:
1. In a large-sized bowl, soak the beans in water overnight. After soaking, drain and rinse, and then transfer into a large-sized Dutch oven. Add water to cover the beans and bring to a simmer. Reduce the heat and cook for 45 minutes or until the beans are tender. When cooked, drain the beans and let cool.
2. While the beans are cooking, grease a small-sized skillet and heat over medium heat. Add the onion and cook, stirring often, for about 7 minutes or until golden.
3. Transfer the onion into the slow cooker. Add the beans into the cooker and stir to combine. Add he barbecue sauce, mango puree, maple syrup, balsamic vinegar, water, bourbon, pepper, chipotle powder, and salt, and stir well until combined.

4. Cover and cook for 6-8 hours on LOW or until the sauce is thick.

Baked Beans

Prep Time: 10 minutes; **Cook Time:** 8 hours on LOW; 4 hours on HIGH	

Serving Size: 106 g; **Serves:** 8; **Calories:** 268

Total Fat: 1.1 g **Saturated Fat:** 0 g; **Trans Fat:** 0 g

Protein: 13.2 g; **Total Carbs:** 53.4 g

Dietary Fiber: 14.7 g; **Sugars:** 17.1 g

Cholesterol: 0 mg; **Sodium:** 116 mg; **Potassium:** 953 mg;

Vitamin A: 10%; **Vitamin C:** 6%; **Calcium:** 12%; **Iron:** 23%

Ingredients:
- ☐ 1 pound dried beans (Great Northern, navy beans, pinto, etc.)
- ☐ 1 onion, medium-sized, diced
- ☐ 1 tablespoon smoked paprika
- ☐ 1 tablespoon white balsamic vinegar or cider vinegar
- ☐ 1 tablespoon vegan Worcestershire sauce
- ☐ 1/3 cup brown sugar
- ☐ 1/3 cup molasses
- ☐ 1/4 cup tomato sauce or ketchup
- ☐ 2 tablespoons yellow mustard
- ☐ Salt and pepper, to taste

Directions:
1. Sort the beans and then rinse. Put into the slow cooker. Add just enough water to cover the beans with 2 inches of water. Let soak overnight.
2. After soaking, drain the beans and return into the slow cooker. Add the rest of the ingredients. Add 2 1/2 cups of fresh water and season with a pinch of salt and pepper.
3. Cover and cook for 8 hours on LOW or for 4 hours on HIGH.
4. Before serving, add seasoning.

Notes: This dish can be made 2 days ahead of time. As a matter of fact, the flavors become more pronounced over time. Keep in the fridge.

Mashed Potatoes

Prep Time: 20 minutes; **Cook Time:** 4 hours on HIGH

Serving Size: 496 g; **Serves:** 4; **Calories:** 312

Total Fat: 10.4 g **Saturated Fat**: 6 g; **Trans Fat**: 0 g

Protein: 9.7 g; **Total Carbs:** 46.6 g

Dietary Fiber: 4.9 g; **Sugars:** 4.1 g

Cholesterol: 24 mg; **Sodium**: 1142 mg; **Potassium**: 1462 mg;

Vitamin A: 6%; **Vitamin C**: 41%; **Calcium**: 6%; **Iron**: 14%

Ingredients:

- ☐ 2 1/2-3 pounds red potatoes, peeled and cut into large-sized chunks
- ☐ 3 tablespoons Earth Balance butter, or your preferred dairy-free butter
- ☐ 1/4 teaspoon black pepper
- ☐ 1/4 cup milk, dairy-free
- ☐ 1 teaspoon sea salt
- ☐ 1 box (24 ounces) vegetable broth PLUS 1/4 cup vegetable broth

Directions:

1. Put the red potatoes into the slow cooker. Pour the broth over the potatoes.
2. Cover and cook for 2 hours on HIGH.
3. When cooked, transfer the potatoes into a large-sized bowl. Transfer the cooking liquid into a heat-safe container and save.
4. Return the potatoes into the slow cooker. Add the vegan butter and then 1/4 cup of the reserved cooking liquid.
5. Using a hand mixer, mix to combine the potatoes with the butter and cooking liquid.
6. Add the soy milk and season with salt and pepper to taste; mix again.
7. Cover and cook for 2 hours on HIGH.
8. If you are keeping it warm, cover and adjust the setting to LOW.
9. When ready to serve, stir the mixture. If the mashed potatoes seem too thick, add more reserved cooking liquid and then mix well.

Notes: You can keep any leftovers in the fridge for 3 days. When ready to serve, just microwave to reheat, stirring occasionally until warmed through. These mashed potatoes can be frozen for up to 4 months. When ready to serve, thaw in the fridge overnight. The mashed potatoes may separate from the liquid. Just mix and reheat in the microwave on HIGH, stirring every 2 minutes until warmed through.

Garlicky Mashed Cauliflower

Prep Time: 20 minutes; **Cook Time:** 4-6 hours on LOW, 2-3 hours on HIGH

Prep Time: 20 minutes; **Cook Time:** 4-6 hours on LOW, 2-3 hours on HIGH

Serving Size: 252 g; **Serves:** 4-6; **Calories:** 47

Total Fat: 3 g **Saturated Fat:** 1.8 g; **Trans Fat:** 0 g

Protein: 1.5 g; **Total Carbs:** 4.5 g

Dietary Fiber: 1.7 g; **Sugars:** 1.6 g

Cholesterol: 8 mg; **Sodium:** 628 mg; **Potassium:** 216 mg;

Vitamin A: 2%; **Vitamin C:** 53%; **Calcium:** 3%; **Iron:** 2%

Ingredients:
- ☐ 1 head cauliflower, cut into florets
- ☐ 1 bay leaf
- ☐ 1 tablespoon Earth Balance buttery spread
- ☐ 1 teaspoon salt
- ☐ 3 cups water
- ☐ 4 garlic cloves, large-sized, peeled
- ☐ Non-dairy milk, if needed
- ☐ Salt and pepper

Directions:
1. Put the cauliflower florets in the slow cooker. Add the garlic cloves, water, bay leaf, and salt.
2. Cover and cook for 2 to 3 hours on HIGH or for 4 to 6 hours on LOW.
3. When cooked, drain the water. Remove the bay leaf and garlic cloves.
4. Add the vegan butter in the cooker and let melt.
5. Mash the cauliflower with a potato masher. Alternatively, you can mash using an immersion blender to make the dish creamier.
6. If needed, add milk by tablespoons until the mixture reaches your desired consistency and then season with salt and pepper to taste. Garnish each serving with green onions or chives. Serve.

Soups, Stews, Chowders, and Chilies

White Bean Soup with Carrots, Sundried Tomatoes, and Potatoes

Prep Time: 0 minutes; **Cook Time:** 0 minutes

Serving Size: 597 g; **Serves:** 6; **Calories:** 403

Total Fat: 3.1 g **Saturated Fat:** 0.7 g; **Trans Fat:** 0 g

Protein: 25.8 g; **Total Carbs:** 69.5 g

Dietary Fiber: 22.9 g; **Sugars:** 10 g

Cholesterol: 0 mg; **Sodium:** 1857 mg; **Potassium:** 1825 mg;

Vitamin A: 261%; **Vitamin C:** 49%; **Calcium:** 17%; **Iron:** 32%

Ingredients:
- ☐ 1 pound dry navy beans, sorted and rinsed
- ☐ 1 pound frozen carrots, sliced
- ☐ 1 cup sun-dried tomatoes, chopped
- ☐ 2 potatoes, medium-sized, diced
- ☐ 1 onion, medium-sized, diced
- ☐ 1/4 teaspoon pepper
- ☐ 1-2 teaspoons dried dill
- ☐ 2 quarts vegetable broth
- ☐ 2 teaspoons salt
- ☐ 3-4 tablespoons fresh parsley, minced
- ☐ 4 cloves garlic, peeled and smashed

Directions:
1. Combine the beans, broth, garlic, onion, salt and pepper in a large slow cooker.
2. Cover and cook for 3-4 hours on LOW or until the beans are soft, but not falling apart. Add additional water, if necessary.
3. Add the potatoes and continue cooking on LOW for about 15-25 minutes or until soft.
4. Add the tomatoes, carrots, and dill. Continue cooking just until the carrots are heated through.
5. Stir in the parsley and, if needed, season with salt and pepper to taste. Serve.

Mushroom Lentil Barley Stew

Prep Time: 15 minutes; **Cook Time:** 4-6 hours on HIGH; 10-12 hours on LOW

Serving Size: 302 g; **Serves:** 8; **Calories:** 184

Total Fat: 1.9 g **Saturated Fat**: 0 g; **Trans Fat**: 0 g

Protein: 12.3 g; **Total Carbs:** 29.8 g

Dietary Fiber: 9.2 g; **Sugars:** 2.3 g

Cholesterol: 0 mg; **Sodium:** 796 mg; **Potassium**: 534 mg;

Vitamin A: 1%; **Vitamin C**: 5%; **Calcium**: 4%; **Iron**: 18%

Ingredients:
- ☐ 3/4 cup pearl barley, uncooked
- ☐ 3/4 cup dry lentils
- ☐ 1 ounce dried shiitake mushrooms, torn into pieces
- ☐ 2 cups fresh button mushrooms, sliced
- ☐ 1 teaspoon dried basil
- ☐ 1/4 cup dried onion flakes
- ☐ 2 quarts vegetable broth
- ☐ 2 teaspoons dried summer savory
- ☐ 2 teaspoons garlic, minced
- ☐ 2 teaspoons ground black pepper
- ☐ 3 bay leaves
- ☐ Salt, to taste

Directions:
1. Put all of the ingredients into the slow cooker and stir to mix.
2. Cover and cook for 4-6 hours on HIGH or for 10-12 hours on LOW.
3. When cooked, remove the bay leaves and discard.
4. Serve the stew.

Tangy Corn, Potato, Soy Milk Chowder

Prep Time: 30 minutes; **Cook Time:** 8 hours on LOW	
Serving Size: 735 g; **Serves:** 6; **Calories:** 741	
Total Fat: 17.2 g **Saturated Fat:** 6.5 g; **Trans Fat:** 0 g	
Protein: 27.1 g; **Total Carbs:** 140.8 g	
Dietary Fiber: 20.7 g; **Sugars:** 25.5 g	
Cholesterol: 20 mg; **Sodium:** 1360 mg; **Potassium:** 2353 mg;	
Vitamin A: 15%; **Vitamin C:** 96%; **Calcium:** 5%; **Iron:** 98%	

Ingredients:

- ☐ 2 cans (12 ounces each) whole kernel corn
- ☐ 3 potatoes, diced
- ☐ 1 3/4 cups soymilk
- ☐ 1/4 cup Earth Balance butter spread
- ☐ 1 tablespoon parsley flakes
- ☐ 1 tablespoon chili powder
- ☐ 1 onion, large-sized, diced
- ☐ 1 lime, juiced
- ☐ 1 clove garlic, minced
- ☐ 2 red chili peppers, minced
- ☐ 2 teaspoons salt
- ☐ 3 cups vegetable broth
- ☐ Black pepper, to taste

Directions:

1. Except for the soy milk, butter, and lime juice, put the rest of the ingredients into the slow cooker.
2. Cover and cook on for 7 hours on LOW.
3. With an immersion blender, puree the mix right in the slow cooker until smooth. Alternatively, you can puree the mix in batches using a blender. If pureed in a blender, return the mix into the slow cooker. Stir in the soy milk and butter. Cook for 1 more hour. Stir in the lime juice. Serve.

Pumpkin, Spinach, Fava Beans, Tomato, Broccoli, Okra, and Zucchini Chili

Prep Time: 25 minutes; **Cook Time:** 3 hours, 20 minutes on LOW

Serving Size: 334 g; **Serves:** 9; **Calories:** 346	
Total Fat: 4.1 g **Saturated Fat:** 1.3 g; **Trans Fat:** 0 g	
Protein: 30.2 g; **Total Carbs:** 50.1 g	
Dietary Fiber: 19.1 g; **Sugars:** 11.7 g	
Cholesterol: 34 mg; **Sodium:** 404 mg; **Potassium:** 1327 mg;	
Vitamin A: 193%; **Vitamin C:** 56%; **Calcium:** 12%; **Iron:** 71%	

Ingredients:

- 1 can (14 ounce) pumpkin, 100% pure
- 1 can (19 ounce) fava beans, drained
- 1 can (28 ounce) diced tomatoes
- 1 carrot, peeled and chopped
- 1 cup broccoli, chopped
- 1 cup okra, chopped
- 2 cups spinach, chopped
- 1 zucchini, small-sized, diced
- 1 package (12 ounce) vegetarian ground beef crumbles
- 1 cup vegetable juice
- 1 onion, small-sized, diced
- 1 teaspoon chili powder, or to taste
- 1 teaspoon salt
- 1/2 teaspoon ground black pepper
- 2 tablespoons pumpkin pie spice
- 2 tablespoons white sugar
- 2 tablespoons white vinegar

Directions:

1. Except for the fava beans, beef crumbles, and spinach, put all of the ingredients into the slow cooker.
2. Cover and cook for 3-4 hours on HIGH.
3. Stir in the beans, beef crumbles, and spinach into the slow cooker.
4. Cook for 20-30 minutes more. Serve.

Black Bean, Kidney Bean, Tomato, Broccoli, Carrot, and Cauliflower Vegetable Soup

Prep Time: 10 minutes; **Cook Time:** 6 hours on HIGH

Serving Size: 663 g; **Serves:** 8; **Calories:** 555

Total Fat: 13.7 g **Saturated Fat:** 2.3 g; **Trans Fat:** 0 g

Protein: 30.8 g; **Total Carbs:** 82.6 g

Dietary Fiber: 21.6 g; **Sugars:** 12.7 g

Cholesterol: 0 mg; **Sodium:** 1291 mg; **Potassium:** 2437 mg;

Vitamin A: 214%; **Vitamin C:** 166%; **Calcium:** 200%; **Iron:** 42%

Ingredients:
- [ ] 1 can (15 ounces) black beans
- [ ] 1 can (12 ounces) kidney beans
- [ ] 1 large can (28 ounces) or 2 cans (14 ounces) seasoned diced tomatoes
- [ ] 16 ounces frozen broccoli cuts
- [ ] 16 ounces frozen carrots
- [ ] 16 ounces frozen cauliflower
- [ ] 12 ounces frozen onions
- [ ] 1/2 teaspoon ground pepper
- [ ] 1 1/2 teaspoons salt
- [ ] 2 1/2 tablespoons dried rosemary
- [ ] 2 tablespoons garlic powder
- [ ] 6 tablespoons olive oil
- [ ] 8 cups vegetable broth

Directions:
1. Put all of the ingredients into a 5-quart or larger-sized slow cooker.
2. Cover and cook for 6 hours on HIGH.
3. Let cool and serve.

Sour and Hot Pea, Bamboo Shoot, Mushroom, and Tofu Soup

Prep Time: 15 minutes; **Cook Time:** 8 hours on LOW

Serving Size: 693 g; **Serves:** 4; **Calories:** 265

Total Fat: 6.9 g **Saturated Fat:** 1.3 g; **Trans Fat:** 0 g

Protein: 18.7 g; **Total Carbs:** 38.9 g

Dietary Fiber: 9.2 g; **Sugars:** 12.5 g

Cholesterol: 0 mg; **Sodium:** 884 mg; **Potassium:** 1055 mg;

Vitamin A: 11%; **Vitamin C:** 47%; **Calcium:** 26%; **Iron:** 33%

Ingredients:
- 1 1/2 cups peas, fresh or frozen
- 1 can (8 ounces) bamboo shoots, drained and julienned
- 1 package (10 ounces) sliced mushrooms
- 1 package (15 ounces) tofu, firm or silken, cubed
- 8 fresh shiitake mushrooms, stems removed and caps sliced
- 1 teaspoon chili paste
- 1 teaspoon sesame oil, plus extra for drizzling
- 2 tablespoons fresh ginger, grated, divided
- 2 tablespoons rice wine vinegar or apple cider vinegar
- 2 tablespoons soy sauce (or tamari or coconut aminos, for gluten-free)
- 2 tablespoons vegan bouillon, chicken-flavored
- 4 cloves garlic, minced
- 4 cups water

Directions:
1. The night before, prepare the bamboo shoots, mushrooms, tofu, ginger, and garlic and store them in airtight containers. Keep in the fridge.
2. In the morning, combine the prepared garlic, tofu, mushrooms, bamboo shoots, and 1 tablespoon ginger, bouillon, water, sesame oil, soy sauce, vinegar, and chili paste in the slow cooker.
3. Cover and cook for 8 hours on LOW.

4. A couple of minutes before serving, add the peas and the remaining 1 tablespoon ginger. Stir to combine. Taste and, if needed, add more vinegar or chili.
5. Drizzle each serving with a few drops of sesame oil.
6. Serve with chili paste on the side for people who like it hot.

Sweet Potato Rice Milk Soup with Spinach and Almonds

Prep Time: 15 minutes; **Cook Time:** 8 hours on LOW; 5 hours on HIGH	

Serving Size: 358 g; **Serves:** 6-8; **Calories:** 188
Total Fat: 4.7 g **Saturated Fat:** 0.6 g; **Trans Fat:** 0 g
Protein: 7.1 g; **Total Carbs:** 29.8 g
Dietary Fiber: 4.6 g; **Sugars:** 2.1 g
Cholesterol: 0 mg; **Sodium:** 777 mg; **Potassium:** 945 mg;
Vitamin A: 21%; **Vitamin C:** 30%; **Calcium:** 6%; **Iron:** 8%

Ingredients:
- ☐ 3 sweet potatoes, large-sized, peeled and chopped
- ☐ 1 cup rice milk, or your preferred
- ☐ 2 cups baby spinach
- ☐ 6-8 tablespoons almonds, sliced
- ☐ 1 cup onion, chopped
- ☐ 1 teaspoon dried tarragon
- ☐ 1 teaspoon McCormick Pinch Perfect Salt Free Seasoning
- ☐ 2 cloves garlic, crushed
- ☐ 2 stalks celery, chopped
- ☐ 5 cups vegetable broth, low sodium
- ☐ Sea salt and ground black pepper, to taste

Directions:
1. Put the sweet potato, garlic, celery, onion, and broth into a 4-quart slow cooker.
2. Cover and cook for 8 hours on LOW or for 5 hours on HIGH, until the potatoes are soft.
3. Turn off the slow cooker. Add the milk, seasoning, and tarragon in the cooker. Using an immersion blender, blend for 1 to 2 minutes until smooth.
4. Stir in the spinach. Cover and let sit for 20 minutes or until the soft.
5. Ladle into soup bowls. Season with salt and pepper to taste. Garnish each serving with 1 tablespoon of sliced almonds.

Notes: If you don't have an immersion blender, carefully ladle 1/3 of the soup into a blender and process until smooth. Pour the pureed soup into a warm holding pot. Repeat the process until all the soup is blended and then return into the slow cooker.

White Bean, Carrot, Celery, Tomato, and Leafy Greens Stew

Prep Time: 20 minutes; **Cook Time:** 3-4 hours on HIGH; 8-10 hours on LOW

Serving Size: 467 g; **Serves:** 10-12; **Calories:** 339	
Total Fat: 1.1 g **Saturated Fat:** 0 g; **Trans Fat:** 0 g	
Protein: 23 g; **Total Carbs:** 62.6 g	
Dietary Fiber: 16 g; **Sugars:** 5.3 g	
Cholesterol: 0 mg; **Sodium:** 1460 mg; **Potassium:** 2023 mg;	
Vitamin A: 116%; **Vitamin C:** 55%; **Calcium:** 28%; **Iron:** 59%	

Ingredients:
- ☐ 2 pounds white beans
- ☐ 5-6 cups leafy greens, roughly chopped, or more, if desired (spinach, chard, kale)
- ☐ 1 can (28 ounces) diced tomatoes, fire-roasted
- ☐ 2 carrots, large-sized, peeled and diced
- ☐ 3 stalks celery, large-sized, diced
- ☐ 3 cloves garlic, minced or chopped
- ☐ 2 tablespoons salt, or to taste
- ☐ 10-12 cups water
- ☐ 1 teaspoon thyme
- ☐ 1 teaspoon oregano
- ☐ 1 teaspoon dried rosemary
- ☐ 1 onion, diced
- ☐ 1 bay leaf
- ☐ Ground black pepper, to taste
- ☐ Polenta, rice, or bread, for serving

Directions:
1. Sort the beans and then rinse a couple of times in a colander under cold running water. Put into the slow cooker. Add the carrots, onion, celery, bay leaf, garlic, and herbs. Add the water – use more water for a more liquid stew or use less for a thicker stew.
2. Cover and cook for 3-4 hours on HIGH or for 8-10 hours on LOW.
3. After cooking time, uncover and add the tomatoes, salt, and pepper; cook for 1 1/2 hours or until the beans are

very soft. Just before serving, add the greens and then stir to combine. Serve.

4. If the beans are already soft after the initial cooking, then add the tomatoes and the greens and then serve immediately.

5. Serve with bread or over polenta or cooked rice.

Indian-Spiced Red Lentil, Spinach, and Coconut Milk Soup

Prep Time: 15 minutes; **Cook Time:** 2 hours on HIGH; 4 hours on LOW, plus 30 minutes on HIGH

Serving Size: 439 g; **Serves:** 4-6; **Calories:** 467	

Serving Size: 439 g; **Serves:** 4-6; **Calories:** 467

Total Fat: 28.2 g **Saturated Fat**: 21.6 g; **Trans Fat**: 0 g

Protein: 17 g; **Total Carbs:** 41.6 g

Dietary Fiber: 19.7 g; **Sugars:** 7.2 g

Cholesterol: 0 mg; **Sodium**: 158 mg; **Potassium**: 959 mg;

Vitamin A: 57%; **Vitamin C**: 27%; **Calcium**: 9%; **Iron**: 38%

Ingredients:

- ☐ 1 to 1 1/2 cup red lentils
- ☐ 1 can (14 ounces) light coconut milk
- ☐ 4 cups fresh spinach, chopped, or more, if desired
- ☐ 1 onion, large-sized, chopped
- ☐ 1 tablespoon olive oil
- ☐ 1 teaspoon ground cinnamon
- ☐ 1 teaspoon ground coriander seed
- ☐ 1 teaspoon ground cumin
- ☐ 1 teaspoon ground turmeric
- ☐ 1/2 teaspoon Garam Masala
- ☐ 2 teaspoons garlic, minced
- ☐ 4 cups vegetable stock
- ☐ Fresh lime, to add at the table, optional
- ☐ Salt and fresh ground black pepper, to taste

Directions:

1. In a medium frying pan, heat the oil over medium-high heat. When hot, add the onion and sauté for about 6 to 8 minutes or until beginning to brown.
2. Add the garlic, cinnamon, garam masala, turmeric, coriander, and cumin. Stir and cook for 1 to 2 minutes. Transfer the onion mix into the 5 1/2-quart slow cooker.
3. Pick the lentils, discarding any discolored ones. Put the lentils in a colander and rinse under running cold water until the water is clear. Add into the slow cooker. Add the stock.

4. Close and cook for 2 hours on HIGH or for 4 hours on LOW or until the lentils falls apart.
5. If cooking on HIGH, set the slow cooker to LOW. Add the coconut milk and spinach. Cook for about 30 minutes or until the spinach and the lentils are cooked to your liking.
6. If needed, season with salt and pepper to taste. Serve hot with vegan yogurt or lime slices at the table.

Butternut Squash, Chickpea, and Black Bean Coconut Chili

Prep Time: 10 minutes; **Cook Time:** 4-6 hours on HIGH; 8 hours on LOW

Serving Size: 314 g; **Serves:** 8; **Calories:** 556

Total Fat: 16.7 g **Saturated Fat:** 11.4 g; **Trans Fat:** 0 g

Protein: 24.7 g; **Total Carbs:** 83.1 g

Dietary Fiber: 21.2 g; **Sugars:** 16.8 g

Cholesterol: 0 mg; **Sodium:** 241 mg; **Potassium:** 1746 mg;

Vitamin A: 132%; **Vitamin C:** 32%; **Calcium:** 17%; **Iron:** 45%

Ingredients:
- ☐ 1 can (15 ounces) black beans, drained and rinsed
- ☐ 1 can (400ml) coconut milk, low-fat
- ☐ 1 can (14 ounces) chickpeas, drained and rinsed
- ☐ 1 onion, small-sized, peeled and finely chopped
- ☐ 1 tablespoon ground cumin
- ☐ 1 teaspoon dried oregano
- ☐ 2 apples, medium-sized, peeled and diced
- ☐ 2 carrots, peeled and chopped
- ☐ 2 cups butternut squash, peeled and diced
- ☐ 2 cups vegetable broth
- ☐ 2 stalks celery, chopped
- ☐ 2 tablespoons tomato paste
- ☐ 2 teaspoons chili powder
- ☐ 4 cloves garlic, peeled and finely minced (OR 1 teaspoon garlic powder)
- ☐ Salt and pepper, to taste

For serving:
- ☐ Fresh cilantro, chopped, OR parsley, OR chives, for garnish
- ☐ Shredded coconut, unsweetened, for garnish
- ☐ Basmati rice, cooked, optional

Directions:
1. Put all of the ingredients in the slow cooker.
2. Cover and cook for 4-6 hours on HIGH or for 8 hours on LOW.

3. During the last hour of cooking, taste, and if needed, season with salt and pepper. If desired, add more chili powder. If you want more spice, add a pinch of cayenne pepper.
4. During the last 45 minutes of cooking, open the lid to allow evaporation of liquid to thicken the chili. If the chili is too dry, add more vegetables to the broth.
5. Serve over hot cooked basmati rice. Garnish each serving with shredded coconut and fresh herbs.

Curried Chickpea, Cauliflower, Potato, and Spinach Vegetable Stew

Prep Time: 30 minutes; **Cook Time:** 4 hours on HIGH	

Serving Size: 471 g; **Serves:** 8-10; **Calories:** 583

Total Fat: 15.4 g **Saturated Fat:** 7.3 g; **Trans Fat:** 0 g

Protein: 27.4 g; **Total Carbs:** 90.4 g

Dietary Fiber: 24.7 g; **Sugars:** 20.5 g

Cholesterol: 0 mg; **Sodium:** 1142 mg; **Potassium:** 1980 mg;

Vitamin A: 105%; **Vitamin C:** 180%; **Calcium:** 20%; **Iron:** 54%

Ingredients:
- ☐ 1 bag (10 ounces) baby spinach
- ☐ 1 can (28 ounces) diced tomatoes with their juices
- ☐ 2 cans (15.5 ounces each) chickpeas, drained and rinsed
- ☐ 2 red or yellow potatoes, medium-sized, diced
- ☐ 1 head cauliflower, medium-sized, cut into bite-sized florets
- ☐ 1 cup coconut milk
- ☐ 1 green bell pepper, diced
- ☐ 1 large onion, diced
- ☐ 1 red bell pepper, diced
- ☐ 1 tablespoon brown sugar
- ☐ 1 tablespoon curry powder
- ☐ 1 tablespoon kosher salt
- ☐ 1 teaspoon olive oil
- ☐ 1/4 teaspoon black pepper
- ☐ 1/8 teaspoon cayenne pepper, optional
- ☐ 1-inch piece ginger, peeled and grated (about 1 tablespoon)
- ☐ 2 cups vegetable broth
- ☐ 3 cloves garlic, minced

Directions:
1. Over medium heat, heat the oil in a skillet. Add the onion, season with 1 teaspoon of salt, and sauté for about 5 minutes or until the onion is translucent.

2. Add the diced potatoes, season with another 1 teaspoon salt, and sauté until the edges of the potatoes are translucent.
3. Stir in the cayenne, garlic, ginger, sugar, brown sugar, and curry; stir for about 30 seconds or until fragrant.
4. Pour 1/4 cup of broth into the skillet to deglaze, scraping the browned bits off from bottom. Transfer the mixture into a 6-quart or larger-sized slow cooker.
5. Add the cauliflower, chickpeas, bell pepper, tomatoes with its juices, 1 teaspoon of salt, pepper, and the remaining broth. Stir to combine. The cooking liquid should reach halfway up the sides of the slow cooker. If needed, add more broth.
6. Cover and cook on HIGH for 4 hours.
7. Stir in the coconut milk and the spinach. Cover for a couple of minutes to let the spinach wilt. Taste and, if needed, season with more salt and other seasonings.
8. Serve over orzo pasta, Israeli couscous, couscous, or serve on its own.

Sweet Potato, Quinoa, and Black Bean Chili

Prep Time: 15 minutes; **Cook Time:** 8-10 hours on LOW; 5-6 hours on HIGH	
Serving Size: 404 g; **Serves**: 6; **Calories:** 479	
Total Fat: 3.7 g **Saturated Fat**: 0.8 g; **Trans Fat**: 0 g	
Protein: 27.6 g; **Total Carbs**: 88.3 g	
Dietary Fiber: 20.4 g; **Sugars**: 10.3 g	
Cholesterol: 0 mg; **Sodium**: 683 mg; **Potassium**: 2236 mg;	
Vitamin A: 48%; **Vitamin C**: 120%; **Calcium**: 16%; **Iron**: 47%	

Ingredients:
- 3 cups black beans, cooked (about 2 cans 15-ounce each, drained)
- 1/2 cup quinoa, uncooked, rinsed well in cool water
- 2 sweet potatoes, medium-sized, peeled and diced
- 2 cans (14-ounce each) diced tomatoes
- 1 green bell pepper, diced
- 1 jalapeno pepper, seeds removed and mince
- 1 tablespoon chili powder
- 1 teaspoon kosher salt
- 1 yellow onion, medium-sized, diced
- 1/4 teaspoon cayenne pepper, less or more to taste
- 1/4 teaspoon smoked paprika
- 2 cups vegetable broth
- 2 tablespoons cocoa powder
- 2 teaspoons cumin
- Salt and pepper, to taste

Toppings:
- Cilantro
- Vegan yogurt (coconut or soy milk)
- Cashew sour cream
- Vegan cheese, shredded
- Green onions, chopped

Directions:
1. Put all the ingredients in a 3-quart or a larger-sized slow cooker.
2. Cover and cook for 8-10 hours on LOW or for 5-6 hours on HIGH.

3. If desired, season with salt and pepper to taste.
4. Serve with your choice of assorted toppings.

Notes: This dish can be stored in the fridge for up to 3 days.

Mango-Black Bean Caribbean Chili

Prep Time: 15 minutes; **Cook Time:** 8-10 hours on LOW; 4-6 hours on HIGH	
Serving Size: 310 g; **Serves:** 6; **Calories:** 586	
Total Fat: 2.9 g **Saturated Fat:** 0.7 g; **Trans Fat:** 0 g	
Protein: 30.8 g; **Total Carbs:** 116 g	
Dietary Fiber: 24.1 g; **Sugars:** 30.3 g	
Cholesterol: 0 mg; **Sodium:** 222 mg; **Potassium:** 2525 mg;	
Vitamin A: 35%; **Vitamin C:** 88%; **Calcium:** 20%; **Iron:** 44%	

Ingredients:

- ☐ 4 cups black beans, cooked (or 2 [15-ounce cans] black beans, drained)
- ☐ 2 cups diced ripe mango (from about 2 large mangoes)
- ☐ 2 (14.5-ounce) cans fire-roasted diced tomatoes (or plain diced tomatoes)
- ☐ 3 cloves garlic, medium-sized, minced
- ☐ 1/4 teaspoon allspice
- ☐ 1/2 teaspoon smoked paprika
- ☐ 1/2 teaspoon kosher salt
- ☐ 1/2 teaspoon cinnamon
- ☐ 1/2 cup orange juice (I use fresh-squeezed from about 2 medium naval oranges)
- ☐ 1/2 cup golden raisins
- ☐ 1 teaspoon cumin
- ☐ 1 tablespoon chili powder
- ☐ 1 medium yellow onion, diced (about 2 cups)
- ☐ 1 jalapeno pepper, diced
- ☐ Salt and pepper, to taste

Toppings:

- ☐ Lime wedges
- ☐ Avocado, diced
- ☐ Scallions, sliced
- ☐ Mango, chopped
- ☐ Cherry tomatoes, halved
- ☐ Cilantro

Directions:

1. Except for the mangoes, put all of the ingredients in a 3-quart or larger-sized slow cooker. Gently stir until combined.
2. Cover and cook for 8-10 on LOW or for 4-6 hours on HIGH.
3. When the cooking time is up, stir in the mango chops. Cover and cook for10 minutes or until the mangoes are warmed. If needed, season with extra salt and pepper.
4. Scoop into serving bowls and top with your choice of toppings.

Vegetarian Cauliflower Buffalo Chili

Prep Time: 15 minutes; **Cook Time:** 8-10 hours on LOW	

Prep Time: 15 minutes; **Cook Time:** 8-10 hours on LOW
Serving Size: 339 g; **Serves:** 6; **Calories:** 527
Total Fat: 2.9 g **Saturated Fat:** 0 g; **Trans Fat:** 0 g
Protein: 33.1 g; **Total Carbs:** 99.1 g
Dietary Fiber: 39.1 g; **Sugars:** 18.5 g
Cholesterol: 0 mg; **Sodium:** 776 mg; **Potassium:** 2554 mg;
Vitamin A: 131%; **Vitamin C:** 94%; **Calcium:** 22%; **Iron:** 69%

Ingredients:

- ☐ 4 cups cannellini beans, cooked (or 2 15-ounce cans, drained)
- ☐ 1/2 medium-sized head cauliflower (about 4 cups florets)
- ☐ 1 can (28-ounce) diced tomatoes, with juice
- ☐ 1 can (4-ounces) fire-roasted diced green chilies
- ☐ 1 onion, medium-sized, diced (about 2 cups)
- ☐ 1 tablespoon chili powder
- ☐ 1/2 cup Frank's Red Hot sauce
- ☐ 1/2 teaspoon kosher salt, or more to taste
- ☐ 1/8 teaspoon cayenne pepper, or more to taste
- ☐ 2 tablespoons brown sugar
- ☐ 2 teaspoons cumin

Toppings:
- ☐ Vegan feta cheese (I used soy feta)
- ☐ Celery, diced
- ☐ Red onion, diced
- ☐ Scallions, sliced
- ☐ Cashew sour cream,
- ☐ Cashew cheddar cheese, shredded

Directions:
1. Put all of the ingredients into a 3-quart or a larger-sized slow cooker. Stir to combine.
2. Cover and cook for 8-10 hours on LOW. Taste and, if needed, season with additional salt.
3. Serve with your choice of toppings.

Notes: This dish can be stored in an airtight container and kept in the fridge for 2 to 3 days or frozen in the freezer for up to 3 months.

Butternut Squash, Carrot, Apple, and Coconut Milk Soup

Prep Time: 25 minutes; **Cook Time:** 6 hours on LOW

Serving Size: 250 g; **Serves:** 8; **Calories:** 183

Total Fat: 12.1 g **Saturated Fat:** 10.3 g; **Trans Fat:** 0 g

Protein: 4 g; **Total Carbs:** 17.8 g

Dietary Fiber: 3.9 g; **Sugars:** 8 g

Cholesterol: 0 mg; **Sodium:** 607 mg; **Potassium:** 547 mg;

Vitamin A: 215%; **Vitamin C:** 30%; **Calcium:** 5%; **Iron:** 10%

Ingredients:

- [ ] 1 butternut squash, medium-sized, (1 pound when peeled and cubed)
- [ ] 1 can (13.5 ounces) coconut milk
- [ ] 1 granny smith apple, peeled and sliced
- [ ] 1/2 pound carrots, peeled and cut into chunks
- [ ] 1 bay leaf
- [ ] 1 onion, medium-sized, diced
- [ ] 1 teaspoon pepper
- [ ] 1 teaspoon salt
- [ ] 1/4 teaspoon dried ground sage
- [ ] 3 cups vegetable broth
- [ ] Salt and pepper, to taste

Directions:

1. Combine the squash with the carrots, apple, onion, bay leaf, and broth in the slow cooker.
2. Cover and cook for 6 hours on LOW or until the vegetables are soft.
3. When cooked, remove and discard the bay leaf.
4. Transfer the cooked mixture into a blender and process until smooth. Alternatively, you can use an immersion blender and puree the mixture right in the slow cooker.
5. If processed in a blender, return the pureed mixture into the slow cooker. Add the coconut milk, sage, salt, and pepper. Stir to combine. Taste and, if needed, season with more salt and pepper to taste.
6. Serve with crusty bread or croutons.

Hearty Slow-Cooker Bulgur Chili

Prep Time: 15 minutes; **Cook Time:** 8 hours on LOW	

Prep Time: 15 minutes; **Cook Time:** 8 hours on LOW

Serving Size: 375 g; **Serves:** 6; **Calories:** 582

Total Fat: 3 g **Saturated Fat:** 0.5 g; **Trans Fat:** 0 g

Protein: 34.6 g; **Total Carbs:** 108.8 g

Dietary Fiber: 26.9 g; **Sugars:** 10.4 g

Cholesterol: 0 mg; **Sodium:** 375 mg; **Potassium:** 2351 mg;

Vitamin A: 34%; **Vitamin C:** 68%; **Calcium:** 18%; **Iron:** 58%

Ingredients:

- ☐ 3/4 cup bulgur wheat
- ☐ 1 can (14 ounces) diced tomatoes
- ☐ 1 can (14 ounces) kidney beans, drained
- ☐ 1 can (14 ounces) pinto beans, drained
- ☐ 1 cup coffee, strong brewed
- ☐ 2 cups white button mushrooms, sliced
- ☐ 2 cups yellow onion, diced
- ☐ 1 cup vegetable broth
- ☐ 1 tablespoon cocoa powder
- ☐ 1 teaspoon dried oregano
- ☐ 1/2 cup red bell pepper, diced
- ☐ 1/2 teaspoon red cayenne pepper, or to taste
- ☐ 1/2 teaspoon salt, or to taste
- ☐ 2 cloves garlic, minced
- ☐ 2 tablespoons brown sugar
- ☐ 2 tablespoons chili powder
- ☐ 2 teaspoons cumin
- ☐ Bay leaf
- ☐ Fresh ground black pepper

Directions:

1. Put the bulgur into a medium-sized bowl. Pour 2 cups of boiling water over the top of the bulgur. Let soak for 15 minutes. Drain after soaking and then squeeze out excess moisture until the bulgur is dry. Transfer into the slow cooker.
2. Add the rest of the ingredients into the slow cooker.
3. Cover and cook for 8 hours on LOW. After cooking time, add more salt and pepper to taste.

4. When ready to serve, remove the bay leaf and discard.
5. Top with vegan Monterey Jack cheese and vegan sharp cheddar cheese, cashew sour cream, and a bit of cilantro.

Black Bean-Quinoa Chili

Prep Time: 10 minutes; **Cook Time:** 2 1/2-3 hours on HIGH; 5-6 hours on LOW

Serving Size: 471 g; **Serves:** 4-5; **Calories:** 631
Total Fat: 12.4 g **Saturated Fat:** 2.5 g; **Trans Fat:** 0 g
Protein: 33.9 g; **Total Carbs:** 101.3 g
Dietary Fiber: 22.1 g; **Sugars:** 9.8 g
Cholesterol: 0 mg; **Sodium:** 1590 mg; **Potassium:** 2410 mg;
Vitamin A: 139%; **Vitamin C:** 81%; **Calcium:** 20%; **Iron:** 53%

Ingredients:
- 1 can (15 ounces) black beans
- 1/2 of a 28-ounces can diced tomatoes
- 1/2 cup quinoa, uncooked
- 1 1/2 teaspoon salt
- 1 carrot, shredded
- 1 teaspoon ground black pepper
- 1 teaspoon ground cumin
- 1 teaspoon oregano
- 1/2 chili pepper, small-sized
- 1/2 cup corn kernels
- 1/2 onion, chopped
- 1/4 cup green bell pepper, chopped
- 1/4 cup red bell pepper, chopped
- 1/4 teaspoon cayenne pepper
- 2 1/4 cups vegetable broth
- 2 cloves garlic
- 2 teaspoons chili powder

For the vegan cashew sour cream:
- 1/2 cup cashews, soaked in water overnight
- 1 teaspoon lime juice
- 1/2 teaspoon fine sea salt
- 3-4 tablespoons water
- Splash apple cider vinegar

For toppings:
- Avocado chunks

☐ Green onions, chopped
☐ Carrot, shredded

Directions:
For the quinoa:
1. Put all the ingredients into the slow cooker and stir to combine.
2. Cover and cook for 2 1/2-3 hours on HIGH or for 5-6 hours on LOW. If cooking on high, check at the last 30 minutes of cooking time. If cooking on low, check at the last hour of cooking time.

For the vegan cashew sour cream:
1. Put all the ingredients in a high-powered blender, process for about 30 seconds or until smooth. Scrape the blender halfway through processing, if needed.
2. Serve as a topping for the chili with avocado and chopped green onions.

Corn, Potato, Soy Milk, and Red Pepper Chowder

Prep Time: 30 minutes; **Cook Time:** 8-10 hours on LOW; 4-6 hours on HIGH, plus 20-30 minutes on LOW

Serving Size: 539 g; **Serves:** 4-6; **Calories:** 383	
Total Fat: 11.7 g **Saturated Fat:** 1.9 g; **Trans Fat:** 0 g	
Protein: 15.2 g; **Total Carbs:** 61.8 g	
Dietary Fiber: 7.5 g; **Sugars:** 11.7 g	
Cholesterol: 0 mg; **Sodium:** 1415 mg; **Potassium:** 1351 mg;	
Vitamin A: 24%; **Vitamin C:** 152%; **Calcium:** 6%; **Iron:** 36%	

Ingredients:
- [ ] 4 cups sweet corn kernels, frozen, divided (or fresh corn kernel, about 4 ears corn)
- [ ] 3 Yukon Gold potatoes, medium-sized, diced (about 3 cups, or 1 pound)
- [ ] 1 cup soy milk OR almond milk
- [ ] 1 red bell pepper, medium-sized, seeded and diced
- [ ] 1 teaspoon ground cumin
- [ ] 1 teaspoon kosher salt
- [ ] 1 yellow onion, medium-sized, diced (about 2 cups)
- [ ] 1/2 teaspoon smoked paprika
- [ ] 1/8 teaspoon cayenne pepper
- [ ] 2 tablespoons olive oil
- [ ] 4 cups vegetable broth
- [ ] Salt and fresh ground pepper, to taste
- [ ] Corn kernels, chopped red bell pepper, sliced scallions, to garnish

Directions:
1. Pout the olive oil in a sauté pan and heat over medium heat. Add the onion. Cook for about 5 minutes, occasionally stirring, until soft and transparent. Transfer the onion mix into the slow cooker.
2. Add the potatoes, red bell pepper, 1 cup of corn, salt, cayenne pepper, paprika, cumin, broth in the cooker.
3. Cover and cook for 8-10 hours on LOW or for 4-6 hours on HIGH or until the potatoes are tender.
4. Turn off the slow cooker and remove the lid. Let the soup slightly cool. With an immersion blender, puree the soup

until smooth. Alternatively, you can puree the soup in a blender in batches. If pureeing in a blender, return into the slow cooker.

5. Stir the remaining 3 cups of corn and the soy milk into the pureed soup.

6. Cover and cook for 20-30 minutes on LOW or until heated through. Taste and, if needed, season with salt and pepper to taste.

7. Serve. Garnish each serving with extra sliced scallions, diced bell pepper, and/or corn.

Black Bean, Pinto Bean, and Kidney Bean Chili

Prep Time: 20 minutes; **Cook Time:** 6-8 hours on LOW	

Serving Size: 401 g; **Serves:** 8; **Calories:** 811

Total Fat: 6.8 g **Saturated Fat:** 1.1 g; **Trans Fat:** 0 g

Protein: 49 g; **Total Carbs:** 143.6 g

Dietary Fiber: 35.6 g; **Sugars:** 10.8 g

Cholesterol: 0 mg; **Sodium:** 190 mg; **Potassium:** 3552 mg;

Vitamin A: 29%; **Vitamin C:** 45%; **Calcium:** 27%; **Iron:** 74%

Ingredients:

- ☐ 28 ounces canned diced Mexican-style tomatoes
- ☐ 28 ounces canned black beans, drained and rinsed
- ☐ 16 ounces canned pinto beans, drained and rinsed
- ☐ 16 ounces canned kidney beans, drained and rinsed
- ☐ 2 tablespoons oil
- ☐ 2 1/2 teaspoon cumin
- ☐ 1 teaspoon oregano
- ☐ 1 tablespoon soy sauce
- ☐ 1 tablespoon red wine vinegar
- ☐ 1 tablespoon chili powder
- ☐ 1 cup white onion, chopped
- ☐ 1 bay leaf
- ☐ 1 1/2 cups vegetable stock
- ☐ 6 cloves garlic, minced
- ☐ 6 ounces tomato paste
- ☐ Red pepper flakes, to taste
- ☐ 1 pound veggie burger crumbles, optional

Directions:

1. Put the oil in a large-sized skillet and heat over medium heat. Add the onion, garlic, if using, veggie burger crumbles, and pepper flakes. Cook until the onion is soft.
2. Add the cumin and chili powder. Cook for 2 minutes more or until fragrant. Transfer into the slow cooker. Add the remaining ingredients in the cooker and stir to combine.
3. Cover and cook for 6-8 hours on LOW.
4. Garnish each serving with vegan sour cream, vegan cheddar cheese, and chopped chives.

Brown Lentil, Potato, Carrot, and Chard Soup

Prep Time: 20 minutes; **Cook Time:** 8 hours on LOW

Serving Size: 389 g; **Serves:** 6; **Calories:** 276

Total Fat: 4.2 g **Saturated Fat:** 0.8 g; **Trans Fat:** 0 g

Protein: 16.2 g; **Total Carbs:** 44.6 g

Dietary Fiber: 12.3 g; **Sugars:** 3.9 g

Cholesterol: 0 mg; **Sodium:** 950 mg; **Potassium:** 1104 mg;

Vitamin A: 42%; **Vitamin C:** 45%; **Calcium:** 6%; **Iron:** 22%

Ingredients:
- ☐ 1 carrot, large-sized, sliced
- ☐ 1 cup dried brown lentils, picked over and rinsed
- ☐ 4 Yukon Gold potatoes, medium-sized, cut into 1-inch pieces
- ☐ 1 large bunch of Swiss chard, stems sliced, leaves torn into bite-sized pieces
- ☐ 1 large yellow onion, chopped
- ☐ 1 stalk celery, sliced
- ☐ 1 tablespoon olive oil
- ☐ 1 tablespoon soy sauce or tamari
- ☐ 2 cloves garlic, minced
- ☐ 6 cup vegetable broth
- ☐ Salt and pepper, to taste

Directions:
1. Put the oil in a large-sized skillet and heat over medium heat. Add the celery, onion, garlic, carrot, and Swiss chard stems.
2. Cover and cook for 8-10 minutes or until softened, stirring occasionally. Transfer the mixture into a 4-6 quart slow cooker. Add the potatoes, lentils, soy sauce, and broth into the cooker. Stir to combine. Cover and cook for 8 hours on LOW.
3. Just before the soup is cooked, bring a large pot of water to a boil. Place the chard leaves in the boiling water. Cook for 5 minutes or until tender. Drain well and then stir into the soup. Taste and, if needed, season with salt and pepper.

Sweet Potato, Carrots, and Chickpea Chili

Prep Time: 30 minutes; **Cook Time:** 8-10 hours on LOW	

Serving Size: 371 g; **Serves:** 8; **Calories:** 565

Total Fat: 8.9 g **Saturated Fat:** 0.9 g; **Trans Fat:** 0 g

Protein: 28.9 g; **Total Carbs:** 98.1 g

Dietary Fiber: 27.7 g; **Sugars:** 22.8 g

Cholesterol: 0 mg; **Sodium:** 623 mg; **Potassium:** 1816 mg;

Vitamin A: 88%; **Vitamin C:** 100%; **Calcium:** 18%; **Iron:** 58%

Ingredients:

- ☐ 2 cans (19 ounces each) chickpeas, drained and rinsed
- ☐ 2 carrots, peeled and diced
- ☐ 1 sweet potato, large-sized, peeled and cut into 1 1/2 to inch cubes (about 5 cups cubed)
- ☐ 28 ounces canned diced tomatoes
- ☐ 13.5 ounces canned tomato sauce
- ☐ 1/2 a 6.5 ounces can chipotle peppers in adobo sauce, peppers chopped (about 6 chipotle peppers and 2 tablespoons adobo sauce)
- ☐ 1 teaspoon ground cumin
- ☐ 1 teaspoon salt
- ☐ 1/2 cup vegetable stock
- ☐ 1/2 lime, juiced, after cooking
- ☐ 2 onions, medium-sized, diced
- ☐ 2 tablespoons chili powder
- ☐ 4 cloves garlic, minced

To serve (optional):
- ☐ Avocado
- ☐ Cilantro leaves
- ☐ Vegan yogurt or cashew sour cream
- ☐ Tortilla chips

Directions:
1. Combine the diced tomatoes with the tomato sauce, stock, chipotles, salt, cumin, and chili powder in the slow cooker. Using a spatula, mix well until combined.
2. Add the rest of the ingredients in the cooker and mix.

3. At this point, you can refrigerate the slow cooker bowl overnight until ready to cook.
4. Cover and cook for 8-10 hours on LOW.
5. Serve with tortilla chips, cashew sour cream, vegan yogurt, cilantro, and avocado.

Notes: This dish can be quite spicy. If you don't want a very spicy chili, start with 1 to 2 chipotle peppers. You can even omit them.

Pumpkin Black Bean Chili with Tomato

Prep Time: 10 minutes; **Cook Time:** 8-10 hours on LOW

Serving Size: 448 g; **Serves:** 6; **Calories:** 792

Total Fat: 3.8 g **Saturated Fat:** 1 g; **Trans Fat:** 0 g

Protein: 48.5 g; **Total Carbs:** 147.6 g

Dietary Fiber: 37 g; **Sugars:** 12.2 g

Cholesterol: 0 mg; **Sodium:** 229 mg; **Potassium:** 3690 mg;

Vitamin A: 171%; **Vitamin C:** 104%; **Calcium:** 31%; **Iron:** 68%

Ingredients:
- ☐ 3 cans (15-ounce each) black beans, drained
- ☐ 2 cans (14.5-ounce each) diced tomatoes, plain
- ☐ 1 cup pumpkin puree (not pumpkin pie mix)
- ☐ 2 cups yellow onion, diced (about 1 medium onion)
- ☐ 1 yellow bell pepper, medium-sized, diced
- ☐ 1 tablespoon chili powder
- ☐ 1 teaspoon cinnamon
- ☐ 1 teaspoon cumin
- ☐ 1/4 teaspoon nutmeg
- ☐ 1/8 teaspoon ground cloves
- ☐ 1/2 teaspoon kosher salt
- ☐ 1/2 teaspoon black pepper, coarse ground

Your choice of toppings:
- ☐ Avocado
- ☐ Cashew cheddar cheese
- ☐ Cashew sour cream
- ☐ Cherry tomatoes, chopped
- ☐ Cilantro
- ☐ Onion or scallions
- ☐ Tapatio sauce, for some heat

Directions:
1. Put all of the ingredients into a 4-quart or larger-sized slow cooker. Stir to combine.
2. Cook for 8 to 10 hours on LOW.
3. Serve with your preferred assorted toppings.

Rotini Pasta, Mushroom, Carrot, and Tomato Vegetable Soup

Prep Time: 10 minutes; **Cook Time:** 8 hours on LOW, plus 20-30 minutes on HIGH

Serving Size: 213 g; **Serves:** 15; **Calories:** 61	
Total Fat: 0.7 g **Saturated Fat:** 0 g; **Trans Fat:** 0 g	
Protein: 3.5 g; **Total Carbs:** 10.9 g	
Dietary Fiber: 1.3 g; **Sugars:** 4.6 g	
Cholesterol: 6 mg; **Sodium:** 548 mg; **Potassium:** 406 mg;	
Vitamin A: 40%; **Vitamin C:** 34%; **Calcium:** 2%; **Iron:** 6%	

Ingredients:
- 2 cups rotini pasta, uncooked
- 1 can (28 ounces) diced tomatoes
- 4 cups tomato juice
- 1 cup carrots, sliced
- 1 cup celery, sliced
- 1 cup mushrooms, sliced
- 1 tablespoon dried basil
- 1 teaspoon salt
- 1/2 cup onion, chopped
- 1/4 teaspoon pepper
- 4 cups vegetable broth

Directions:
1. Except for the uncooked pasta and the cheese, put all the ingredients into a 6-quart slow cooker.
2. Cover and cook for 8 hours on LOW.
3. After cooking time, add the pasta and stir. Adjust the setting to HIGH and cook for 20 to 30 minutes or until the pasta is done.

Black Beans, Kidney Beans, Tomato, and Sweet Potatoes Chili

Prep Time: 20 minutes; **Cook Time:** 7-8 hours on HIGH; 4-5 hours on LOW

Serving Size: 253 g; **Serves:** 8; **Calories:** 423	

Serving Size: 253 g; **Serves:** 8; **Calories:** 423

Total Fat: 2 g **Saturated Fat:** 0 g; **Trans Fat:** 0 g

Protein: 26.1 g; **Total Carbs:** 78.8 g

Dietary Fiber: 19.5 g; **Sugars:** 7.3 g

Cholesterol: 0 mg; **Sodium:** 31 mg; **Potassium:** 1957 mg;

Vitamin A: 33%; **Vitamin C:** 86%; **Calcium:** 14%; **Iron:** 45%

Ingredients:

- ☐ 1 can (15.5-ounce) black beans, rinsed
- ☐ 1 can (15.5-ounce) kidney beans, rinsed
- ☐ 1 can (28-ounce) fire-roasted diced tomatoes
- ☐ 1 green bell pepper, chopped
- ☐ 1 red onion, medium-sized, chopped
- ☐ 1 sweet potato, medium-sized, (about 8 ounces), peeled and cut into 1/2-inch pieces
- ☐ 1 tablespoon chili powder
- ☐ 1 tablespoon ground cumin
- ☐ 1/4 teaspoon ground cinnamon
- ☐ 2 teaspoons unsweetened cocoa powder
- ☐ 4 garlic cloves, chopped
- ☐ Kosher salt and black pepper

For serving:
- ☐ Cashew sour cream
- ☐ Scallions, sliced
- ☐ Radishes, sliced
- ☐ Tortilla chips

Directions:
1. Put all the ingredients in a 4-6 quart slow cooker and stir to combine.
2. Cover and cook for 7-8 hours on HIGH or for 4-5 hours on LOW, or until the chili is thick and the potatoes are tender.
3. Serve with suggested serving accompaniments.

Pumpkin, Red Lentil, and Kidney Beans Chili

Prep Time: 10 minutes; **Cook Time:** 4-5 hours on HIGH; 8-10 hours on LOW
Serving Size: 462 g; **Serves:** 6; **Calories:** 660
Total Fat: 3.2 g **Saturated Fat:** 0.6 g; **Trans Fat:** 0 g
Protein: 44.2 g; **Total Carbs:** 118.8 g
Dietary Fiber: 35.5 g; **Sugars:** 10 g
Cholesterol: 0 mg; **Sodium:** 685 mg; **Potassium:** 2814 mg;
Vitamin A: 159%; **Vitamin C:** 54%; **Calcium:** 18%; **Iron:** 77%

Ingredients:
- ☐ 1 cup dry red lentils
- ☐ 1 cup pumpkin puree
- ☐ 2 cans (15-ounce) fire-roasted diced tomatoes
- ☐ 2 cans (15-ounce each) kidney beans, drained
- ☐ 1/8 teaspoon cloves
- ☐ 1/2 teaspoon cinnamon
- ☐ 1 teaspoon kosher salt
- ☐ 1 tablespoon cocoa powder
- ☐ 1 tablespoon chili powder
- ☐ 1 jalapeno pepper, medium-sized, minced (seeds removed, if desired)
- ☐ 1 cup yellow onion, chopped, (about 1/2 of a medium-sized onion)
- ☐ 2 cups vegetable broth
- ☐ 2 teaspoons cumin

Assorted toppings (optional);
- ☐ Tomatoes, diced
- ☐ Onions, diced
- ☐ Cashew sour cream
- ☐ Vegan cheddar cheese, shredded

Directions:
1. Put all of the ingredients into a 3-quart or larger-sized slow cooker.
2. Cook for 4-5 hours on HIGH or for 8-10 hours on LOW until the lentils are tender and the chili is hearty and thick.
3. If desired, serve with your choice of assorted toppings.

Brown Rice and Black Bean Soup

Prep Time: 20 minutes; **Cook Time:** 6-8 hours on LOW, plus 30 minutes on HIGH

Serving Size: 556 g; **Serves:** 6; **Calories:** 1268	
Total Fat: 9.2 g **Saturated Fat:** 2 g; **Trans Fat:** 0 g	
Protein: 70.1 g; **Total Carbs:** 231.5 g	
Dietary Fiber: 46.8 g; **Sugars:** 9 g	
Cholesterol: 0 mg; **Sodium:** 750 mg; **Potassium:** 4684 mg;	
Vitamin A: 67%; **Vitamin C:** 9%; **Calcium:** 40%; **Iron:** 91%	

Ingredients:

- ☐ 4 cans (15-ounces) black beans, drained, but not rinsed (reserve 1 can for the end of the process)
- ☐ 1 cup carrot, diced, (about 2 medium-sized carrots)
- ☐ 2 cups brown rice, cooked
- ☐ 1 cup yellow onion, diced (about 1/2 of a medium-sized onion)
- ☐ 1 jalapeno pepper, medium-sized, seeded and then finely diced (about 1/4 cup)
- ☐ 1 tablespoon garlic, minced (about 2 to 3 medium-sized cloves)
- ☐ 1 tablespoon olive oil
- ☐ 1 teaspoon chili powder
- ☐ 1 teaspoon cumin
- ☐ 1 teaspoon dried oregano
- ☐ 1/2 teaspoon kosher salt plus, more to taste if desired
- ☐ 1/4 teaspoon black pepper, fresh ground
- ☐ 10 dashes Tabasco sauce, or to taste
- ☐ 2 tablespoons tomato paste
- ☐ 4 cups vegetable broth
- ☐ Fresh sliced lime wedges

Toppings:
- ☐ Tomatoes, diced
- ☐ Cilantro leaves
- ☐ Scallions, diced
- ☐ Avocado
- ☐ Cashew sour cream

Directions:
1. Pour 3 cans of the black beans in a 3-quart or larger-sized slow cooker.
2. Put the olive oil into a large-sized sauté pan over medium heat. Add the carrots and onion. Sauté for 5 minutes or until the onion begins to become translucent. Add the garlic, jalapeno, cumin, chili powder, oregano, pepper, and salt; stir and sauté for 1 minute.
3. Stir in the broth, tomato paste, and Tabasco sauce until the tomato paste is dissolved. Pour the mixture over the beans in the slow cooker.
4. Cover and cook for 6-8 hours on LOW.
5. Uncover and let cool slightly until safe to handle. With the immersion blender, puree the soup directly in the slow cooker until smooth. Alternatively, you can puree in batches using a blender. If pureed in a blender, return the pureed soup in the slow cooker. Add the rice and the remaining can of beans. Cook for 30 minutes more on HIGH.
6. If needed, adjust salt and pepper to taste and, if desired, add more Tabasco.
7. Scoop into serving bowls and serve each with a lime wedge on top.
8. Add your choice of toppings.

Notes: This dish can be stored in an airtight container and kept the fridge for 3-4 days. Leftovers thicken over time, so add vegetable broth when reheating leftovers.

5-Ingredient Butternut Squash Thai Curry Soup

Prep Time: 15 minutes; **Cook Time:** 8-10 hours on LOW; 4-6 hours on HIGH, plus 30 minutes on LOW

Serving Size: 482 g; **Serves:** 6; **Calories:** 317	
Total Fat: 19.2 g **Saturated Fat:** 15 g; **Trans Fat:** 0 g	
Protein: 7.2 g; **Total Carbs:** 34 g	
Dietary Fiber: 6.4 g; **Sugars:** 8.4 g	
Cholesterol: 0 mg; **Sodium:** 1112 mg; **Potassium:** 1137 mg;	
Vitamin A: 482%; **Vitamin C:** 85%; **Calcium:** 13%; **Iron:** 20%	

Ingredients:

- ☐ 1 piece (3-pound) butternut squash, peeled, seeded, and then diced (about 8 cups diced squash)
- ☐ 1 can (14-ounce) coconut milk, full fat
- ☐ 1 yellow onion, medium-sized, diced
- ☐ 1/2 teaspoon kosher salt , plus more to taste
- ☐ 3 tablespoons Thai red curry paste, less or more to taste
- ☐ 4 cups vegetable broth, low sodium

Optional toppings:
- ☐ Lime wedges, for squeezing over the top
- ☐ Hot red pepper, thinly sliced
- ☐ Fresh cilantro
- ☐ Extra drizzle coconut milk

Directions:

1. Put the squash, broth, onion, and 1/2 teaspoon of salt into a 4-quart or larger-sized slow cooker. Stir to combine.
2. Cover and cook for 8-10 hours on LOW or for 4-6 hours on HIGH.
3. Uncover and let the soup cool slightly. When cool enough to handle, puree right in the slow cooker using an immersion blender. Alternatively, you can puree in batches using a blender. If pureed in a blender, return the pureed soup in the slow cooker. Stir in the curry paste and coconut milk.
4. Cover and cook for 30 minutes more or LOW or until the soup is reheated.
5. Taste and add more salt and curry paste, if desired.

6. Serve as is or with your choice of toppings.

Vegetable Mixed Bean Soup

Prep Time: 10 minutes; **Cook Time:** 4-5 hours on HIGH, 6-8 hours on LOW

Serving Size: 378 g; **Serves:** 6; **Calories:** 156

Total Fat: 3 g **Saturated Fat:** 0.6 g; **Trans Fat:** 0 g

Protein: 9.6 g; **Total Carbs:** 22.5 g

Dietary Fiber: 3.6 g; **Sugars:** 3.8 g

Cholesterol: 0 mg; **Sodium**: 922 mg; **Potassium**: 559 mg;

Vitamin A: 138%; **Vitamin C**: 12%; **Calcium**: 6%; **Iron**: 14%

Ingredients:

- 1 1/2 cups bean and grain soup mix (I used Pereg)
- 1 onion, large-sized, chopped
- 1 tablespoon fresh thyme, minced
- 4 carrots, medium-sized, scrubbed and chopped
- 4 cloves garlic, large-sized, minced
- 7 cups vegetable stock, low-sodium
- Fresh sliced lemon wedges, for squeezing on top, optional
- Salt and black pepper

Directions:

1. The night before, put the soup mix into a bowl of cold water and let soak overnight.
2. The next morning, drain and rinse the soup mix.
3. Except for the lemon wedges and thyme, put all of the ingredients into the slow cooker. Stir to combine. Start with 1/4 teaspoon of black pepper and 1/2 teaspoon of salt, adding more as needed later.
4. Cover and cook for 4-5 hours on HIGH. Do not open to check until 4 hours into cooking. Alternatively, you can cook for 6-8 hours on LOW, checking at the 6th hour of cooking.
5. When the cooking time is up, stir in the thyme. Taste and season with more salt and pepper as needed.
6. Top each serving with fresh-sliced lemon wedges.

Chinese-Inspired Hot Pot

Prep Time: 30 minutes; **Cook Time:** 7-8 hours on LOW, plus 20 minutes on LOW

Serving Size: 525 g; **Serves:** 6-8; **Calories:** 187		

Serving Size: 525 g; **Serves:** 6-8; **Calories:** 187

Total Fat: 3.3 g **Saturated Fat**: 0.6 g; **Trans Fat**: 0 g

Protein: 8.9 g; **Total Carbs:** 33.3 g

Dietary Fiber: 4.9 g; **Sugars:** 6.6 g

Cholesterol: 0 mg; **Sodium:** 947 mg; **Potassium**: 726 mg;

Vitamin A: 88%; **Vitamin C**: 51%; **Calcium**: 15%; **Iron**: 17%

Ingredients:
For the soup:
- ☐ 8 ounces canned sliced water chestnuts, drained
- ☐ 8 ounces canned bamboo shoots, drained
- ☐ 60 ounces vegetable stock
- ☐ 3 tablespoons soy sauce, low sodium
- ☐ 2 teaspoons ginger paste
- ☐ 2 teaspoons garlic paste
- ☐ 2 stalks celery, cut into diagonal slices
- ☐ 1/2 teaspoon red pepper flakes, or to taste
- ☐ 1 yellow onion, mediums-sized, chopped
- ☐ 1 cup carrot, cut into diagonal slices

Additions:
- ☐ 8 ounces firm tofu, drained and cubed
- ☐ 6 scallions, chopped and divided
- ☐ 4 ounces button mushrooms, sliced
- ☐ 2 bunches baby bok choy, sliced
- ☐ 1 ounce snow peas, strings removed, cut into 1-inch pieces

For the ginger soy sauce:
- ☐ 2 tablespoons soy sauce, low sodium
- ☐ 2 tablespoons ginger paste
- ☐ 2 tablespoons agave syrup
- ☐ 1 teaspoon sesame oil

Directions:
1. Put all the soup ingredients into a large-sized slow cooker.

2. Cover and cook for 7-8 hours on LOW.
3. About 20 minutes before serving, add the additions into the slow cooker. Add only 1/2 of the scallions, reserving the other half for garnishing.
4. Cover and cook for 20 minutes more.
5. Meanwhile, combine all of the sauce ingredients in a small-sized bowl, whisking until well combined.
6. Ladle the soup into serving bowls, scooping 1 spoonful of sauce into each serving. Garnish with the remaining scallions. Serve immediately.

Desserts

Hot Chocolate Pudding Cake

Prep Time: 30 minutes; **Cook Time:** 1 1/2 hours on HIGH, plus 1 hour sitting

Serving Size: 377 g; **Serves:** 3; **Calories:** 533

Total Fat: 33 g **Saturated Fat:** 27.5 g; **Trans Fat:** 0 g

Protein: 10.8 g; **Total Carbs:** 69.2 g

Dietary Fiber: 18.7 g; **Sugars:** 11.8 g

Cholesterol: 0 mg; **Sodium:** 806 mg; **Potassium:** 1204 mg;

Vitamin A: 0%; **Vitamin C:** 6%; **Calcium:** 17%; **Iron:** 36%

Ingredients:
- [ ] 1 1/2 cups almond milk or your choice of non-dairy milk
- [ ] 1 3/4 teaspoon baking powder
- [ ] 1 cup spelt, all-purpose, or Bob's gluten-free flour
- [ ] 1 teaspoon instant coffee powder, optional
- [ ] 1 teaspoon salt
- [ ] 1/2 cup cocoa powder
- [ ] 1/2 cup mini chocolate chips, optional
- [ ] 2 1/2 teaspoon pure vanilla extract
- [ ] 2 cups boiling water
- [ ] 2 tablespoon applesauce OR 2 tablespoon more oil
- [ ] 2 tablespoons coconut or vegetable oil
- [ ] 3/4 cup sugar, your choice or xylitol (I used 2 teaspoons liquid stevia)
- [ ] Pinch pure stevia OR 2 tablespoon brown or coconut sugar

Directions:
1. Grease the bowl of the slow cooker and set aside.
2. In a large-sized mixing bowl, mix the flour with the salt, baking powder, cocoa powder, sweetener of choice, and, if using, coffee powder.
3. In another bowl, whisk the almond milk with the applesauce, oil, vanilla, and, if using, warmed coconut oil.
4. Pour the wet ingredients into the dry ingredients, stirring until combined evenly. Pour the mixture into the slow

cooker. Pour the boiling water over the top – DO NOT STIR.

5. Close and cook for 1 1/2 hours on HIGH. Turn the slow cooker off and slightly open the lid; let sit for 1 hour to let the cake thicken further.

6. This dessert resembles pudding during the first day. If you let it completely cool and refrigerate all night, it will get creamier and thicker.

Apple Crisp

Prep Time: 20 minutes; **Cook Time:** 4 hours on LOW

Serving Size: 127 g; **Serves:** 8; **Calories:** 300

Total Fat: 9.4 g **Saturated Fat:** 4.4 g; **Trans Fat:** 0 g

Protein: 2.8 g; **Total Carbs:** 55.1 g

Dietary Fiber: 4.9 g; **Sugars:** 37.8 g

Cholesterol: 17 mg; **Sodium:** 73 mg; **Potassium:** 248 mg;

Vitamin A: 4%; **Vitamin C:** 25%; **Calcium:** 3%; **Iron:** 10%

Ingredients:
- [ ] 6 cups apples, chopped
- [ ] 4 1/2 tablespoons Earth Balance butter spread
- [ ] 3/4 cup brown sugar, packed
- [ ] 3/4 cup all-purpose flour
- [ ] 2 tablespoons fresh squeezed lemon juice
- [ ] 2 tablespoons apple pie spice, divided
- [ ] 1/4 cup white sugar
- [ ] 1/4 cup walnuts, chopped
- [ ] 1 tablespoon corn starch
- [ ] 1 tablespoon apple butter
- [ ] Dash salt
- [ ] Vegan ice cream, for garnish

Directions:
1. Put the apple into the slow cooker. Add the lemon juice and apple butter. Stir to coat.
2. In a bowl, mix the white sugar, 1 tablespoon of apple pie spice, and cornstarch until well combined. Pour the sugar mix over the apples in the slow cooker and then stir to coat.
3. Add the walnuts and mix until well combined.
4. In a new bowl, mix the flour with the remaining 1 tablespoon of apple pie spice, brown sugar, and salt. With a pastry cutter, cut the butter into the flour mix until the mixture resembles crumbly sand. Sprinkle the mix over the apple mixture in the cooker.
5. Cover and cook for 4 hours on LOW or until the apples are soft and tender.

Peanut Butter-Triple Chocolate Pudding Cake

Prep Time: 20 minutes; **Cook Time:** 2-2 1/2 hours on HIGH, plus 30-40 minutes cooling

Serving Size: 159 g; **Serves:** 8; **Calories:** 432		
Total Fat: 21.1 g **Saturated Fat:** 6.3 g; **Trans Fat:** 0 g		
Protein: 10.1 g; **Total Carbs:** 55.6 g		
Dietary Fiber: 3.6 g; **Sugars:** 37.8 g		
Cholesterol: 8 mg; **Sodium:** 103 mg; **Potassium:** 419 mg;		
Vitamin A: 1%; **Vitamin C:** 0%; **Calcium:** 10%; **Iron:** 19%		

Ingredients:
- 1 cup all-purpose flour
- 2 tablespoons cocoa powder, unsweetened
- 1/3 cup sugar
- 1/2 cup chocolate milk (I used almond breeze)
- 2 tablespoons vegetable oil
- 2 teaspoons vanilla
- 1/2 cup peanuts, chopped
- 1/2 cup chocolate pieces, semisweet
- 1/2 cup peanut butter-flavor pieces
- Nonstick cooking spray

For the topping:
- 1 1/2 cups boiling water
- 1 1/2 teaspoons baking powder
- 2 tablespoons cocoa powder, unsweetened
- 3/4 cup sugar

For serving:
- Chocolate bar pieces, optional
- Vanilla ice cream, optional

Directions:
1. Lightly grease a 3 ½- to 4-quart slow cooker with nonstick cooking spray or line your cooker with disposable liner.
2. For the flour mix, stir the flour with the sugar, cocoa powder, and baking powder in a medium-sized bowl. Add the milk, vanilla, and oil, and stir until just moistened.

Stir in the peanuts, chocolate pieces, and peanut butter pieces. Spread the batter evenly into the prepared slow cooker.

3. In a different medium-sized bowl, combine the cocoa powder with the sugar. Stir the boiling water in the mix gradually. Carefully pour the mixture over the batter in the slow cooker.

4. Cover and cook for 2-2 1/2 hours on HIGH or until a toothpick comes out clean when inserted in the center of the cake.

5. Turn off the slow cooker. Remove the liner and transfer into a heat safe surface. Let stand uncovered for about 30-40 minutes to slightly cool.

6. When slightly cool, spoon the cake onto dessert dishes. Top with chocolate pieces or ice cream, if desired.

Scalloped Peaches

Prep Time: 0 minutes; **Cook Time:** 0 hours

Serving Size: 132 g; **Serves:** 8; **Calories:** 204

Total Fat: 6.2 g **Saturated Fat:** 3.6 g; **Trans Fat:** 0 g

Protein: 1.5 g; **Total Carbs:** 39.2 g

Dietary Fiber: 2.4 g; **Sugars:** 39 g

Cholesterol: 15 mg; **Sodium:** 41 mg; **Potassium:** 289 mg;

Vitamin A: 13%; **Vitamin C:** 16%; **Calcium:** 0%; **Iron:** 2%

Ingredients:
- ☐ 8 peaches, sliced
- ☐ 1/4 cup Earth Balance butter, sliced
- ☐ 1/2 teaspoon ground cloves
- ☐ 1/2 teaspoon ground cinnamon
- ☐ 1 cup sugar
- ☐ Vegan vanilla ice cream, for serving

Directions:
In the bowl of a 4 quart slow cooker, combine the peaches, sugar, cinnamon, cloves and butter. Toss lightly to combine. Cover and cook on low for 1 1/2 to 2 hours. Serve hot with a scoop of vanilla ice cream.

Lemon Blueberry Cake

Prep Time: 15 minutes; **Cook Time:** 60-80 minutes on HIGH	

Serving Size: 50 g; **Serves**: 4; **Calories:** 123

Total Fat: 6.3 g **Saturated Fat:** 4.4 g; **Trans Fat:** 0 g

Protein: 2.3 g; **Total Carbs:** 14.8 g

Dietary Fiber: 1.3 g; **Sugars:** 1.7 g

Cholesterol: 0 mg; **Sodium:** 4 mg; **Potassium**: 114 mg;

Vitamin A: 0%; **Vitamin C:** 4%; **Calcium:** 2%; **Iron:** 8%

Ingredients:

For the dry ingredients:
- ☐ 1/2 cup whole-wheat pastry flour
- ☐ 1/4 teaspoon baking powder
- ☐ 1/4 teaspoon stevia (plus 1 teaspoon agave nectar or sweetener of your choice), to taste

For the wet ingredients:
- ☐ 1 teaspoon ground flaxseeds, mix with 2 teaspoons warm water
- ☐ 1 teaspoon olive oil (pumpkin purée or applesauce)
- ☐ 1/2 teaspoon lemon zest
- ☐ 1/3 cup non-dairy milk, unsweetened
- ☐ 1/4 teaspoon lemon extract
- ☐ 1/4 cup blueberries
- ☐ 1/4 teaspoon vanilla extract

Directions:

1. Grease a 1 1/2-2 quart slow cooker with oil, or line with parchment paper or slow cooker liner.
2. In a bowl, mix all of the dry ingredients. In a different bowl, mix all of the wet ingredients.
3. Add the wet mixture into the dry mixture until combined.
4. Pour the mixture into the prepared slow cooker, spreading evenly onto the bottom.
5. Put a paper towel or a clean dishtowel over the slow cooker opening and then cover with its lid. The towel will absorb the condensation and prevent it from dripping onto the cake.

6. Cook for 60-80 minutes on HIGH or until the center of the cake is firm and does not indent when touched.

Almond and Coconut Rice Pudding

Prep Time: 15 minutes; **Cook Time:** 4 hours on LOW; 2-2 1/2 hours on HIGH

Serving Size: 247 g; **Serves:** 4-5; **Calories:** 624	

Serving Size: 247 g; **Serves**: 4-5; **Calories:** 624

Total Fat: 42.9 g **Saturated Fat:** 35.5 g; **Trans Fat:** 0 g

Protein: 7.3 g; **Total Carbs:** 60.7 g

Dietary Fiber: 5.8 g; **Sugars:** 16.8 g

Cholesterol: 0 mg; **Sodium:** 43 mg; **Potassium:** 658 mg;

Vitamin A: 0%; **Vitamin C**: 9%; **Calcium**: 7%; **Iron**: 24%

Ingredients:
- ☐ 1 can (14 ounces) light coconut milk
- ☐ 1 cup almond milk, unsweetened vanilla or your choice of non-dairy milk
- ☐ 1/2 cup basmati rice OR brown or white rice
- ☐ 1/2 cup raisins
- ☐ 1/2 teaspoon ground cinnamon
- ☐ 1/2 teaspoon vanilla extract
- ☐ 1/4 cup agave nectar, divided
- ☐ 1/4 cup almonds, chopped and toasted
- ☐ 1/4 cup shredded coconut
- ☐ 1/4 teaspoon almond extract
- ☐ 1/4 teaspoon ground nutmeg
- ☐ 1/4-1/2 cup water, less or more for desired consistency

Directions:
1. Turn on the slow cooker.
2. Put the rice, almond milk, coconut milk, almond extract, vanilla extract, nutmeg, and cinnamon into the slow cooker. If the mixture needs more liquid, add a bit more water.
3. Cover and cook for 4 hours on LOW or for 2-2 1/2 hours on HIGH.
4. When the cooking time is up, mix in the shredded coconut, almonds, and raisins.
5. Divide the rice pudding between 4 bowls. Drizzle each serving with 1/2-1 tablespoon agave nectar and then sprinkle the top with a couple of coconut flakes.

Poached Caramel Pears

Prep Time: 15 minutes; **Cook Time:** 2 hours

Serving Size: 268 g; **Serves:** 6; **Calories:** 318

Total Fat: 5.3 g **Saturated Fat:** 3.2 g; **Trans Fat:** 0 g

Protein: 1.3 g; **Total Carbs:** 70.7 g

Dietary Fiber: 6.7 g; **Sugars:** 57.9 g

Cholesterol: 15 mg; **Sodium:** 49 mg; **Potassium:** 326 mg;

Vitamin A: 4%; **Vitamin C:** 15%; **Calcium:** 6%; **Iron:** 4%

Ingredients:
- 6 Bosc pears, peeled, cored, and halved
- 2 tablespoons unsalted butter, cut into small pieces
- 1 tablespoon grated ginger
- 1 pint vegan vanilla ice cream
- 1 1/2 cups dark brown sugar

Directions:
1. Combine the ginger with the sugar and butter in the bowl of a 6-quart slow cooker.
2. Add the pears and toss gently to coat, and then arrange the pears with the cut-side faced down on the slow cooker.
3. Cover and cook for about 1-2 hours on HIGH or until the pears are tender and easily pierced using the tip of a knife.
4. Divide the pears between serving bowls and then divide the ice cream between each serving. Drizzle with the sauce from the slow cooker.

Apple Pie Yellow Cake

Prep Time: 20 minutes; **Cook Time:** 2-3 hours on LOW	

Serving Size: 166 g; **Serves:** 6; **Calories:** 555

Total Fat: 24 g **Saturated Fat:** 11 g; **Trans Fat:** 0 g

Protein: 3.7 g; **Total Carbs:** 85.1 g

Dietary Fiber: 4.4 g; **Sugars:** 55 g

Cholesterol: 42 mg; **Sodium:** 583 mg; **Potassium:** 223 mg;

Vitamin A: 10%; **Vitamin C:** 19%; **Calcium:** 10%; **Iron:** 10%

Ingredients:
- ☐ 4 apples, Granny Smith, peeled and sliced
- ☐ 1/8 teaspoon ground cinnamon
- ☐ 1/4 cup pecans, chopped, optional
- ☐ 1/4 cup coconut sugar
- ☐ 1/2 cup vegan butter, melted (Earth Balance)
- ☐ 1 box yellow cake mix (I use Duncan Hines Moist Deluxe Classic Yellow Cake Mix)

Directions:
1. Use a wide 10-inch diameter slow cooker, if possible, to give the cake a crumbly top. You can use a big oval one, but a regular-sized slow cooker will also work.
2. Line the bottom and the sides of the crockpot with foil – this will prevent the cake from getting to browned and make the cooker easier to clean.
3. Peel and slice the apples. Put the slices into the slow cooker.
4. Mix the cinnamon with the sugar and sprinkle over the apples.
5. Melt the vegan butter for a couple of seconds in the microwave and set aside.
6. Pour the cake mix into a medium bowl. Stir in the butter until well mixed. If needed, use your fingers to pinch and roll to help evenly incorporate the butter and make a crumbly mixture.
7. Sprinkle half of the cake mix over the apples. Stir well to incorporate.
8. Sprinkle the remaining cake mix over the top of the apple mix – do not mix.
9. Cover and cook for 2-3 hours on LOW.

Notes: With a big spoon, spoon the cooked mix into bowls and then sprinkle with chopped pecans.

Conclusion

Thank you again for purchasing this book, I hope you enjoyed reading it as much as I enjoyed writing it for you!

Finally, if you enjoyed this book I'd like to ask you to leave a review for my book on Amazon, it would be greatly appreciated!

All the best and good luck,

Anthony

40099412R00091

Made in the USA
Middletown, DE
03 February 2017